AF544895

AFTERMATH OF HISTORY

THE Aftermath OF THE Sandinista Revolution

STUART A. KALLEN

TWENTY-FIRST CENTURY BOOKS MINNEAPOLIS

Consultant: Dennis Gilbert, Professor of Sociology, Hamilton College, Clinton, NY

The image on the jacket and the cover is of Sandinista rebels raising their rifles in Nicaragua in July 1979. The Sandinistas overthrew the Somoza family dictatorship later that month(Photo © Matthew Naythons/Getty Images).

Twenty-First Century Books
A division of Lerner Publishing Group, Inc.
241 First Avenue North
Minneapolis, MN 55401 U.S.A.

Website address: www.lernerbooks.com

Library of Congress Cataloging-in-Publication Data

Kallen, Stuart A., 1955–
The aftermath of the Sandinista Revolution / by Stuart A. Kallen.
p. cm. — (Aftermath of history)
Includes bibliographical references and index.
ISBN 978-0-8225-9091-0 (lib. bdg. : alk. paper)
1. Nicaragua—Politics and government—1979-1990—Juvenile literature. 2. Nicaragua—Politics and government—1990- —Juvenile literature. 3. Nicaragua—History—Revolution, 1979—Juvenile literature. 4. Frente Sandinista de Liberación Nacional—History—Juvenile literature. I. Title.
F1528.K35 2009
972.8505'3—dc22 2008025356

Manufactured in the United States of America
1 2 3 4 5 6 - BP - 14 13 12 11 10 09

Contents

The Sandinistas Triumph

FOR A FEW WEEKS in the summer of 1979, the Central American Republic of Nicaragua held the center stage in world affairs. On July 19, a group of heavily armed revolutionaries from the Sandinista National Liberation Front (Frente Sandinista de Liberación Nacional, or FSLN) advanced on the capital city of Managua. The brutal government of the Somoza family, which had ruled the nation for decades, was overthrown after a bloody civil war. Nicaragua's feared military force, the National Guard (Guardia Nacional, or GN), collapsed. According to Archbishop Miguel Obando y Bravo, "Military vehicles were driving wildly through the . . . city streets. Guardia Nacional soldiers . . . were throwing their uniforms and military gear into a huge bonfire. Their faces spoke of fear and shame, defeat and exile. . . . The same people who days earlier swore they would kill me, looked at me today with eyes that begged mercy."

The disintegration of the National Guard astonished even the guerrilla fighters (unofficial military groups) of the FSLN. GN officials had controlled Nicaragua through political detention, torture, and execution for decades. However, as the Sandinista army encircled Managua, the only official government authority still at work was the chief of the transit police.

Throughout July 19 and 20, tens of thousands of joyous citizens poured into the streets to hug the triumphant Sandinista guerrillas and thank them for defeating the dictator. Describing the scene, *New York Times* reporter Stephen Kinzer wrote, "The . . . idealism that radiated from their faces was a perfect counterpoint to the aura of corruption . . . that had hung over Nicaragua for so long."

Huge crowds in Managua, Nicaragua, on July 20, 1979, celebrate the victory of the Sandinista guerrillas over the Somoza family dictatorship.

"Our Wildest Dreams"

At the height of the celebration, a shiny red fire engine roared into Managua's central square, quickly renamed the Plaza of the Revolution. Aboard were five members of the Sandinista military command who had been fighting the National Guard since the early 1970s. Much to their surprise, they discovered that they were in absolute control of Nicaragua. Commenting on this situation, military veteran Oscar René Vargas recalled, "We assumed we were going to have to negotiate with the Guard. But . . . we found ourselves in complete command. It was a better situation than we had imagined in our wildest dreams."

This small group of men and women had lived as outlaws for years. But at this moment, they were entering the Presidential Palace in their military fatigues. The FSLN promised to end the widespread poverty that gripped Nicaragua. Euphoria and optimism filled the streets.

For many in the United States, the Sandinista victory was a cause for dread. The movement was founded on Communist ideology. Many Americans feared that the Sandinista victory would allow the powerful Communist Soviet Union to establish a foothold in Central America. This would permit them to spread an anti-American message throughout the region. Hostility toward the United States would threaten U.S. corporations that owned banks, oil companies, and giant farms in Central America.

As the Sandinista government formed in Nicaragua, the revolutionaries found themselves facing a bigger enemy than Somoza. Within a few years, the FSLN would be fighting a war against soldiers trained and financed by the United States, a counterrevolutionary army called the Contras. The Sandinista struggle for their revolutionary cause would become a battle for their survival.

CHAPTER 1

Sandino and the Sandinistas

THE SANDINISTA REVOLUTION was an armed conflict between the Sandinista National Liberation Front and the Nicaraguan Guardia Nacional. The revolution lasted from early 1977 to July 1979, when the Sandinistas triumphed. Conflict between revolutionaries and the government was fairly common throughout Nicaraguan history. From its founding in 1821, the Republic of Nicaragua was regularly entangled in bloody wars. Nicaraguan poet and playwright José Coronel Urtecho noted, "The history of Nicaragua is the history of civil war."

Because of this history of unrest, the United States had been involved with Nicaraguan affairs for years. The United States had played a major role in choosing Nicaraguan leaders and keeping them in power. They did this mainly to protect U.S. corporations that had operations in the country. U.S. Marines were stationed in the country almost continuously from 1912. By the 1920s, however, U.S. anxieties about Nicaragua were driven by events that happened thousands of miles away.

Nicaragua

THE REPUBLIC OF NICARAGUA is the largest nation in Central America and the least populated. From 1980 to 1990, the decade after the Sandinista revolution, the population of the country increased from about 2.5 million to 3.3 million. The country, about the size of New York State, is bordered by Honduras to the north and by Costa Rica to the south. The Pacific Ocean is to the west of the country, and the Caribbean Sea and Atlantic Ocean lie to the east.

Nicaragua was originally named for its indigenous people, the Nicaro. This word was joined with the Spanish word for water, *agua*. The Spaniards probably added *agua* because of the large lakes, Lago de Nicaragua and Lago de Managua, located in the southwest region of the country. Managua is the capital of Nicaragua and its largest city.

The Communist Threat

In March 1917, a populist uprising toppled the imperial government of Czar Nicholas II in Russia. Then, in October 1917, this government was replaced by a government led by Vladimir Ilyich Lenin. Russia's new leaders based their revolution on the *Communist Manifesto*, written in 1848 by German intellectuals Karl Marx and Friedrich Engels. In the book, they write about average workers, called the proletariat, and their struggles with factory and farm owners, called the ruling class, or bourgeoisie. Marx and Engels believed that the proletariat should take control of all factories and farms, referred to as the means of production. Under Marxism, there would be no ruling class. Everyone in society would be equal. All workers would share equally in profits made through the means of production.

Those who believed in Marxism strongly opposed U.S. capitalism. Under the North American system, people are rewarded for their individual accomplishments. Some earn great profits, while others live in the middle or lower classes.

Lenin openly stated that he wanted to spread Marxist Communism throughout the world under the red flag of the Soviet Union, a union of fifteen republics including Russia. By the 1920s, Communism had became a powerful symbol of fear in the United States. Corporate leaders and politicians worried that Marxist ideology would inspire peasant rebels in Nicaragua to seize the banks, plantations, and railroads and turn them into worker-owned enterprises. If this happened, the Communist revolution might spread from Nicaragua throughout Central and South America, threatening international shipping through the Panama Canal to the south. Therefore, U.S. policy experts thought it best to support pro-U.S. governments in Nicaragua.

Political Warfare

Marxism was not the only threat to U.S. interests in Nicaragua. In addition, the country's two powerful political parties were constantly at war with each other. The Liberal Party was made up of ranchers and coffee exporters. Wealthy landowners dominated the Conservative Party. The Conservatives won most elections between the 1850s and the 1920s. The Liberal Party occasionally gained power. Both

parties, led by dictatorial strongmen called caudillos, maintained their own armies. After most elections, the loser challenged the results with armed violence.

In 1925 the Liberal Party began a rebellion known as the Constitutionalist War. U.S. Marines attempted to stop this civil war while U.S. diplomats tried to negotiate a peace settlement. In 1928 Liberals and Conservatives agreed to sign a peace treaty. It was called the Pact of Espino Negro because it was negotiated under the shade of an *espino negro*, a blackthorn tree. Part of the peace agreement required the United States to establish a Nicaraguan army called the Guardia Nacional to prevent another civil war. Retired U.S. Army major Calvin B. Carter was hired to create the guard.

The United States supervised the 1928 election in Nicaragua.

Although a candidate from the Liberal Party won, the Conservatives accepted the outcome. U.S. leaders were pleased because the regime pledged to uphold U.S. interests. The Liberals also promised to repress Marxism. Commenting on the election, U.S. secretary of state Robert Olds noted, "There is no room for any outside influences other than ours in this region. We could not tolerate such a thing without incurring great risks."

After the 1928 election, the United States remained in control of Nicaragua through the U.S. marines and the National Guard. U.S.

Liberals and Conservatives

THE TERMS *LIBERAL* AND *conservative* are often associated with the Democratic and Republican parties in the United States. However, in Nicaragua, members of both the Liberal Party and Conservative Party supported brutal dictators. They also engaged in bloody struggles, keeping Nicaragua in a state of nearly constant civil war since the 1840s. Both parties based political beliefs on money and power. Neither represented the vast majority of Nicaraguans, who lived in poverty.

The two parties trace their roots back to the eighteenth century, a time when Spanish settlers controlled Nicaragua. The Conservative Party consisted of owners of large estates. These people supported strict rules limiting trade and resisted business competition from outsiders. Liberals were mainly business and professional people, not landowners. They supported free-trade policies and resented taxes, tariffs, and trade restrictions that the Conservatives placed on crops and export items.

The violent rivalry between the Liberals and Conservatives lasted well into the twentieth century and remained one of the most important and destructive features of Nicaraguan society. Politicians frequently put their party interests over the well-being of the nation. The impoverished Nicaraguan people were the losers in this political strife.

corporations ran the banking system and the nation's railways. This did not please all Americans, however. U.S. senator Burton Wheeler of Montana said U.S. policy "has led to an armed intervention in Nicaragua in behalf of an American-made puppet-President, foisted upon the people against their own will for the simple reason that he is ready at whatever cost to Nicaragua to serve the New York bankers who . . . have been mercilessly exploiting Nicaragua."

The General of Free Men

Wheeler's words were echoed in speeches made by Augusto César Sandino, a rebel leader. Sandino opposed U.S. imperialism—U.S. military and economic intervention in Nicaraguan affairs.

Sandino, born in 1895, had ties to both the rich and poor in Nicaragua. His father was a wealthy landowner, and his mother was an indigenous laborer in the fields of his father's estate. During the Constitutionalist War, Sandino worked in a U.S.-owned gold mine. He saw workers who labored for very low wages for a powerful corporation. Sandino began to preach Marxism to workers and urged them to change the political system. Putting his words into action, Sandino organized his own independent army of peasants and workers. Armed only with long knives called machetes, they began to fight government forces.

After the Liberals and Conservatives agreed to the peace settlement in 1928, Sandino's army continued their fight. Their cause soon grew from a partisan battle to a war of national liberation. Young supporters looked to Sandino as a symbol of resistance to U.S. imperialism. They gave him the nickname the General of Free Men. When U.S. Marine captain Gilbert Hatfield tried to persuade Sandino to

General Augusto César Sandino *(center)* poses with his staff in 1929. Sandino waged a war against Nicaragua's National Guard and U.S. Marines from 1928 to 1933.

surrender in 1928, Sandino told the marine commander, "I want a free homeland or death." These bold words were adopted as a slogan by Sandino's followers.

Tacho Takes Over the Guard

Sandino waged a guerrilla war against the marines and National Guard from 1928 to 1933. During that time, he built up a fighting force of six thousand men called the Army for the Defense of the National Sovereignty. They marched under a black and red flag. The charismatic Sandino often rallied his followers with Marxist philosophy, stating, "Very soon we shall have our victory in Nicaragua. . . . With it the fuse of a 'proletarian explosion' will be lit against imperialists of the world."

Sandino's army controlled large sections of Nicaragua for five years. His group minted its own money and ran radio and telephone networks. The rebels also instituted social and political changes. They forced large landowners to pay their workers higher wages and provide unemployment benefits. In some areas, the army set up collective farms—enterprises where peasant workers share the profits. The army also formed classes to teach the people to read and write.

Despite Sandino's popularity, the marines continued to pursue him. In areas controlled by his rebel army, marines burned crops and forced thousands of peasants to move. The marines also called in air strikes that destroyed entire villages. These tactics alarmed many Americans, who protested U.S. involvement in Nicaragua.

In 1931 U.S. president Herbert Hoover decided to bring the marines home after the 1932 Nicaraguan elections. But before they could leave, he needed to expand the duties of the National Guard so they could control the country. The guard needed a strong leader, and Hoover found one in Anastasio Somoza García.

Anastasio Somoza became chief director of the National Guard in the 1930s.

Widely known by his nickname Tacho, Somoza was born in 1896 to a wealthy coffee planter. As a teenager, Somoza was sent to live with relatives in Philadelphia, Pennsylvania. There he met his future wife, Salvadora Debayle Sacasa, a

Spanish Names

LIKE MOST PEOPLE OF Spanish heritage, Anastasio Somoza García is known by the first of his two last names. In Spanish-speaking countries, children are customarily given both their father's and mother's last names. However, people are commonly referred to by their father's last name—in this case, Somoza.

member of one of Nicaragua's wealthiest families. After returning to Nicaragua, Somoza fought on the side of the Liberals in the Constitutionalist War. He was awarded the rank of general. By the time he was appointed *jefe director*, or chief director, of the National Guard, Somoza had served as Nicaragua's minister of war and minister of foreign relations. Both jobs allowed him to become very friendly with powerful U.S. officials.

As chief director of the National Guard, Somoza had to negotiate a peace settlement with Sandino. Sandino was willing to stop fighting because his main demand had been satisfied—the marines left Nicaragua after turning over power to Somoza on January 1, 1933. However, Somoza believed that Sandino had political ambitions and would someday run for president. Somoza himself had his eye on that job. To eliminate his political rival, Somoza ordered National Guard troops to kidnap Sandino on February 21, 1934. The rebel leader was taken to the Managua airport, executed by firing squad, and buried under the main runway in the middle of the night. Somoza was not finished eliminating the Marxist opposition. During the following three years, the National Guard hunted down Sandino's supporters, burned their villages, and massacred thousands of sympathizers and their families.

A New Somoza Takes Power

By 1936 Somoza was ready to take power in Nicaragua. He rigged an election in which he received 99 percent of the vote and was inaugurated on January 1, 1937. During the nineteen years that followed, Somoza ruled by keeping a tight control over the National Guard and bribing his political opponents to offer only token resistance. He never gave up his role as chief director of the GN and used the soldiers as a combined police force, army, and spy agency. Guard members often used detention, brutal torture, and assassination to rid the president of his enemies.

Somoza allowed the GN to control government-owned enterprises. GN members ran the national radio and telephone networks, the postal service, health services, the internal revenue service, and

The Power of the National Guard

ANASTASIO SOMOZA CONTROLLED NICARAGUA through his role as chief director of the Guardia Nacional. The National Guard acted as Nicaragua's police, military, intelligence, and customs officers. And the GN was able to maintain power for more than four decades by controlling nearly every aspect of Nicaraguan life. Guard members limited access to information by taking command of the post office, the telegraph service, radio stations, and newspapers. By controlling the immigration department, they were able to limit who was allowed to enter and leave the country. National Guard oversight of the customs bureau prevented importation of guns, ammunition, and gunpowder, which might be used by insurgents. Even the national sanitation service was under the control of the National Guard, which allowed them to discreetly dispose of bodies. With the GN holding control, rebel leaders realized they would have to defeat this powerful force before they could overthrow Somoza.

the national railroads. Guard members also controlled many illegal enterprises including prostitution, gambling, and drug smuggling.

With the GN running the country, Somoza took control of many businesses in Nicaragua by the 1940s. He amassed a fortune of more than $60 million and was the richest man in the region. However, Somoza's widespread corruption created many enemies. On September 21, 1956, the president was shot four times by a twenty-seven-year-old poet, Rigoberto López Pérez, a member of the Nicaraguan Socialist Party (PSN). The president's bodyguards immediately killed the assassin.

U.S. president Dwight D. Eisenhower, who called Somoza a "great friend of the United States," had the Nicaraguan leader flown to a U.S. military hospital for treatment. But Somoza died four days later.

The assassination did not end the Somoza era in Nicaragua. Even as the dictator lay dying, his son Luis Somoza Debayle had taken the reigns of power. Within a few months, Luis had arranged to be formally elected president through an election rigged by his brother Anastasio Somoza Debayle.

Anastasio, nicknamed Tachito, or Little Tacho, was born in 1925. He attended school in the United States and graduated from the U.S. Military Academy at West Point in 1946. The next year, his father made him chief director of the National Guard. According to a joke popular in Nicaragua, Tachito "was the only cadet from the academy ever to be given an army as a graduation present."

The First Sandinistas

Under Tachito's command, the corruption and repression of the National Guard continued to grow. Peasants were beaten for minor crimes. Members of the Conservative Party disappeared or were murdered in front of their families. Nevertheless, a group of students at the University of Nicaragua in Managua began to secretly organize against the regime. These young men and women were inspired by events taking place in Cuba, an island not far from Nicaragua.

In the late 1950s, Cuban Marxist rebels led by Fidel Castro waged a war to overthrow the brutal dictator Fulgencio Batista. On January 1, 1959, Castro's revolutionaries were successful. In Nicaragua, according to Conservative newspaper *La Prensa*, Castro's victory "was met with celebration and widespread joy."

Carlos Fonseca Amador, a member of the Nicaraguan Socialist Party, was one of the celebrants. Because of his political connection to the Socialists, Fonseca had been arrested and tortured following the assassination of Anastasio Somoza. Although Fonseca had no knowledge of the assassination plot, he was held for two months without charges.

In 1957 Fonseca had traveled to the Soviet Union, where he studied Marxist philosophy. After Castro's victory in Cuba, he decided to form a new political organization. This group would lead a rebellion in Nicaragua. For inspiration, Fonseca studied the speeches and writings of Sandino and Ernesto "Che" Guevara. Che was an Argentine-born Marxist revolutionary who took part in the Cuban revolution. Fonseca was particularly interested in Che's lessons from the Cuban revolution.

"The peasant must always be helped technically, economically, morally, and culturally . . . the guerrilla fighter will be a sort of guiding angel who has fallen into the zone [countryside], helping the poor always."

—Che Guevara, Marxist revolutionary, on the principles of waging a revolution, 1961

Che wrote that revolutionary forces could claim victory as long as the insurgents had popular support. Because the police and military forces were concentrated in the cities, Che recommended that insurgents mobilize in the countryside. To attract followers, the guerrillas should help farmers and promote programs based on agricultural reform.

Fonseca dreamed of a revolution based on the ideas of Che and Sandino. He began to recruit members for a new group and made plans to move into the countryside. Fonseca called his organization the National Liberation Front (known by its Spanish acronym FLN for Frente de Liberación Nacional). Founding members included students Silvio Mayorga, Tomás Borge Martínez, Jorge Navarro, and about twenty others. In 1963 Fonseca decided to honor Sandino and show solidarity with his anti-imperialist cause by adding "Sandinista" to the group's name. This created the Frente Sandinista de Liberación Nacional. By this time, the FSLN was growing rapidly in the cities, recruiting students through a group called the Revolutionary Student Front.

During the early years of the FSLN, the organization temporarily seized radio stations to broadcast their messages. They organized strikes to create havoc on the economy, and they robbed supermarkets and banks to finance their activities. In preparation for a guerrilla war against the government, some members of the FSLN traveled to Cuba for training. However, the National Guard was merciless when dealing with FSLN members. Many were tortured, killed, imprisoned, or forced into exile.

The Somoza brothers continued to maintain a tight grip on Nicaraguan society, and Fonseca's group could claim little in the way of success. But the dream of rebellion that Sandino had planted in the 1920s was growing, and the Sandinista revolutionaries refused to surrender to Somoza or his dreaded National Guard.

CHAPTER 2

The Revolution

DURING THE 1960S, Nicaragua was in turmoil. The Sandinistas were organizing on college campuses. Revolutionaries were living in the countryside, where they recruited peasants to their cause. And the Somoza dynasty was nearing its third decade of repressive family rule.

Luis Somoza was running Nicaragua, but he was often troubled by poor health. His brother Tachito had been using the National Guard as his own private police force for nearly twenty years and, for all practical purposes, was the person who controlled Nicaragua. In early 1967, Tachito decided to step out from behind the scenes and become the officially elected president.

The Sandinistas and other government opponents did not want another Somoza to take power and held a preelection protest rally on January 22, 1967. Sixty thousand people took to the streets of

Tachito Somoza speaks at a political rally in Managua in January 1967.

Managua, where opposition politicians gave fiery speeches. When the crowd started marching to the National Palace, National Guard troops opened fire with machine guns. Forty people were killed, and hundreds more were wounded. A tank appeared on the street and began firing rounds into a nearby hotel where opposition leaders were staying. Several weeks later, on February 5, 1967, Tachito Somoza was elected president of Nicaragua in what nonpartisan observers called a blatantly rigged election. Two months later, forty-four-year-old Luis was dead after a massive heart attack.

Corruption and Abuse of Power

President Somoza retained his position as chief director of the National Guard. He looted the national treasury and used the money to take over many businesses in Nicaragua. His family and friends held monopolies in construction, meatpacking, tobacco production, fishing, canning, and automobile sales. Others who wanted to run businesses were forced to pay bribes for operating licenses.

Somoza also tightened his grip on Nicaraguan agriculture. He confiscated peasant farms and turned them into giant agribusiness operations. This move left about 70 percent of Nicaragua's farmland in the hands of less than 3 percent of the population. Deprived of their land, most Nicaraguan farmers were unable to produce enough food for their own use. As a result, starvation was widespread.

Under Somoza's rule, the average individual income in Nicaragua fell to new lows. The typical citizen lived on about $300 a year. This resulted in high infant mortality rates and low life expectancy for adults. Meanwhile, the Somoza family fortune continued to grow. By the early 1970s, it had reached the equivalent of $400 million.

Somoza's corruption created widespread discontent in the countryside. This allowed the FSLN to gain support among the peasantry. Members of the rebel group in northcentral Nicaragua gained the trust of locals. According to FSLN commander Henry Ruiz:

> To win over the peasantry it was necessary to live as a part of it. That is what we did—lived with the campesino [peasant farmer], lived his problems, became one more member of his family. . . . All their reluctance ended when we made ourselves their brothers. By 1972 we had won their confidence totally, and we built an organizational network.

The National Guard attempted to stop the FSLN gains with brutal repression in areas where the guerrillas were present. Peasants were randomly arrested, tortured, and murdered, especially young men of fighting age. Although repressive tactics did prevent large numbers of peasants from joining the FSLN, the policies also helped to increase hatred toward the Somoza regime. Meanwhile, in Managua, a burgeoning student movement was engaged in nearly full-time protests against the government.

The City Crumbles

Somoza's opponents could not stop him from running for president again in 1971. Although this was a violation of the Nicaraguan constitution, which mandated a limit of two terms, Somoza forced opposition leaders to amend the constitution so he could stay in power. As a concession, he agreed to leave office in May 1972. At that time, a handpicked three-member junta, or ruling council, took over the government. Somoza continued to maintain power behind the scenes as chief director of the National Guard.

Somoza's ruling junta was barely seven months old when disaster struck Nicaragua. At seven minutes past midnight on December 23, 1972, the Christmas Earthquake instantly leveled six hundred blocks in central Managua. The disaster killed at least twenty thousand people and destroyed about 75 percent of the houses in Managua along with 90 percent of the city's commercial capacity. The United Nations conservatively estimated the damage to be equal to about $3 billion dollars.

The Nicaraguan earthquake was one of the most devastating natural disasters in modern times. Within hours, money, food, and medical supplies began pouring into Nicaragua from across the globe.

The Christmas Earthquake

ON DECEMBER 23, 1972, a major earthquake struck Managua. U.S. journalist Jay Mallin was a witness to the devastation. His report is excerpted below:

> The quake centered in downtown Managua. For a radius of one to two miles [2 to 3 kilometers] . . . there is not a building that has not been destroyed or damaged. . . .
>
> Just a block off Avenida Central was the market. Here Managua obtained most of its food. Fruits, vegetables, sugar cane, meats, live poultry were available in abundance, and you could also buy clothing, leather goods, religious statues, cutlery and bottles of strange liquids. . . . Now the market is no more.
>
> Bodies are being burned in the streets to avert diseases. The smell of death is abroad, especially near crumbled homes. Sirens are heard constantly. There has been looting, and on one or two occasions even soldiers have been seen helping themselves.

THIS AERIAL VIEW SHOWS THE DAMAGE TO THE DOWNTOWN AREA OF MANAGUA AFTER THE 1972 EARTHQUAKE.

Such charitable feelings were nowhere to be found in the government, however. The National Guard suffered a complete breakdown of discipline. Officers were seen leading soldiers on looting missions while ignoring the dead and wounded that lay in the rubble-strewn streets.

To restore order, Somoza was forced to turn to the U.S. military. But this only made the situation worse. With the Americans in charge, National Guard members had more time to steal relief supplies from warehouses and docks. To the astonishment of observers, these goods were given to family members who sold them from shops set up in empty storefronts. For example, the wife of a military commander ran a black-market store described by an unnamed witness:

> You can buy anything from a small electric generator to a water purifier, electric torches [flashlights], pickaxes and spades, complete factory-sealed blood transfusion equipment. There are also shops selling goods looted from warehouses. . . . Toilet fittings, furniture, street-lights, [and] electric wiring.

Average citizens were left to dig out the dead and wounded from collapsed buildings.

The earthquake also exposed Somoza's blatant corruption. He appointed himself head of the National Emergency Committee, formed to aid earthquake victims. In this position, he took control of all rebuilding efforts. Somoza companies were in charge of construction of temporary housing and demolition work. They sold real estate and building materials. To maintain power, the president diverted aid money from the United States to pay for construction of luxury housing for GN officers. Managua's homeless were given cheap wooden shacks to live in.

"The Peoples' Patience Is Reaching Its Limit"

Although Nicaragua received more than $100 million in international aid for earthquake relief, very little went to the suffering of the poor. Even Somoza's supporters began to resent him after he pushed them aside in order to take control of the construction and banking industries. As a result, young people from elite backgrounds began to sympathize with homeless earthquake victims who flocked to the Sandinistas.

In December 1974, a newly strengthened FSLN carried out a spectacular operation led by Eduardo Contreras Escobar. Several days after Christmas, fifteen guerrillas burst into the house of the minister of agriculture during a party. They killed the minister and took several leading Nicaraguan officials and Somoza relatives hostage. Somoza

Daniel Ortega Saavedra was one of the prisoners released when the FSLN carried out a hostage operation in 1974.

was forced to negotiate a peaceful settlement. He agreed to the demands of the guerrillas, paying them a million dollars in ransom. He also agreed to release fourteen Sandinista prisoners from jail. Among them was the FSLN fighter Daniel Ortega Saavedra.

As part of the negotiations, Somoza agree to allow an official FSLN statement to be broadcast over the radio and printed in *La Prensa*. It read, in part, "The peoples' patience is reaching its limit. . . . At present, the daily plight of the peasantry can be summarized as misery, hunger, malnutrition, fear, night blindness [from lack of a healthy diet], premature death, and illiteracy." The communiqué also mentioned that the average worker earned one dollar a day while gasoline cost thirty cents per liter. Worse, medicine for dysentery, a disease caused from drinking bad water, cost forty cents.

Two days after the operation, the released prisoners and the kidnappers were flown to Cuba. Thousands of cheering supporters gathered in the street of Managua to see off the Sandinistas.

"Psychopaths and Fools"

Somoza was enraged by the Sandinista hostage operation, saying: "They are cowards, blackmailers, psychopaths, and fools. . . . This is the work of communism equal to the assassination of my father." Somoza also criticized Pedro Joaquín Chamorro, publisher and editor in chief of *La Prensa*, the daily newspaper. Chamorro was a member of the Conservative Party and had printed a series of articles describing Somoza's corruption. These helped build support for the FSLN and attracted negative international attention to the government.

In the wake of the FSLN guerrilla operation, Somoza imposed martial law and press censorship. He ordered the National Guard into the countryside to root out Sandinista sympathizers. The soldiers acted with extreme violence, engaging in looting, rape, torture, arbitrary imprisonment, and summary execution. Among the thousands killed was FSLN founder Carlos Fonseca.

The GN operation took place in areas where Catholic missionaries lived. Many religious officials, including priests and nuns, witnessed the dire human rights abuses. Some wrote detailed reports that were released to the press. After the stories were published in the United States, the U.S. House of Representatives held hearings that focused on the corruption of the Somoza regime. A detailed report released after the hearings called Somoza the worst human-rights violator in the Western Hemisphere.

This report came to the attention of Jimmy Carter, who had been elected U.S. president in November 1976. During the campaign, Carter had promised to place considerable emphasis on human rights throughout Latin America. After his inauguration in January 1977, the president decided to punish Somoza, cutting military and economic assistance to Nicaragua. Six months later, Somoza suffered a heart attack. As he recovered, his own supporters looted the treasury and openly plotted to replace him. It was clear that the president was losing control of his country.

Somoza's problems energized Daniel Ortega, who devised a new revolutionary strategy with his brother Humberto. Rather than fight the established opposition, the Sandinistas decided to reach out to all Somoza's enemies. These included members of the Conservative Party, who were not traditional allies of the Sandinistas. Ortega then formed a group called the Insurrectional Tendency, also known as the Third Way, or Terceristas. In October 1977, the Terceristas aligned themselves with an association of leading Nicaraguan professionals,

"There can be no dialogue with Somoza . . . because he is the principal obstacle to all rational understanding."

—Group of Twelve, an association of leading Nicaraguan professionals, 1981

business leaders, and clergy living in exile in Costa Rica. This group was called El Grupo de los Doce, or the Group of Twelve.

Together, the two groups laid plans to form a provisional government in Costa Rica. In the meantime, the FSLN sought to broaden its popularity by adopting a grassroots religious philosophy known as liberation theology. Ninety-two percent of Nicaraguans were Roman Catholics, and their religious beliefs dominated their culture, language, way of thinking, and outlook. Liberation theology, developed by Jesuit priests after World War II (1939–1945), is based on the belief that Jesus was the liberator of the poor and oppressed and that all Christians are required to work for social and economic justice. This belief meshed nicely with the Marxist beliefs of the Sandinistas. However, since the Catholic hierarchy often supported the Somozas throughout the years, liberation theology was considered quite controversial.

The Sandinistas enlisted powerful religious figures such as Jesuits Fernando Cardenal and Alvaro Arguello to adapt liberation theology to revolutionary purposes. Using Catholic terminology, Jesus was discussed as a revolutionary and representative of all oppressed people. The Virgin Mary was seen as the mother of all revolutionary heroes, and the Eucharist (communion) became the bread produced by liberated workers. The capitalist system was compared to the horrors of hell.

Beginning in the mid-1970s, priests, nuns, and theologians were engaged to preach liberation theology on college campuses and in churches. In this way, Marxism and Catholicism were melded to expand support for the revolution.

The FSLN also worked through grassroots citizen groups known as OPs (Popular Organizations). These groups were promoted by the Sandinistas as a way for average citizens to take part in the revolution. Most OPs were based on the unique social or economic situations of the members. For example, there were OPs for peasants, workers, students, residents of urban neighborhoods, teenagers, and women. Members of these groups organized strikes, demonstrations, and offensive actions against the National Guard.

An Opposition Voice Is Silenced

The importance of the OPs was highlighted by a tragedy that sparked the Sandinista revolution. On January 10, 1978, *La Prensa* editor Chamorro was driving to work through the still rubble-filled streets of downtown Managua. A group of professional assassins opened fire on his car and killed him. Nicaraguans were shocked that Chamorro's voice had been silenced, and his death sparked riots in several cities. Enraged citizens burned Somoza-owned businesses. In the days that followed, the OPs helped organize a general strike, during which 90 percent of Nicaraguan citizens refused to go to work or school. The strike shut down the entire country for ten days. When it finally ended, as historian Thomas Walker writes, "Nicaraguans of all classes had experienced the thrill and surge of pride that came with defying the dictator and were, therefore, in no mood to let things slip back to normal."

Things did not return to normal. In the early summer of 1978, the FSLN developed a national political organization called the United People's Movement, or MPU. The group united factory workers, business leaders, Communists, trade unionists, members of the women's movement, and unemployed peasants under a single political banner. The MPU issued a fifteen-point Immediate Program that called for disbanding the National Guard, seizing Somoza-owned properties, and releasing political prisoners. The MPU also called for the formation of a representative democratic government that would institute basic liberties. These included freedom of the press, freedom of religion, and freedom of assembly.

Operation Pigpen

The FSLN stepped up attacks on National Guard bases. Members organized mass demonstrations and student strikes in major cities. In July 1978, the Terceristas and the Group of Twelve returned to Managua, where they were greeted as heroes.

On August 22, the Terceristas staged a dramatic mission called Operation Pigpen. This was designed to weaken Somoza, unite Nicaraguans, and capture international attention. Twenty-three Tercerista commandos led by Edén Pastora, nicknamed Commander Zero, seized the entire Nicaraguan congress while it met in the National Legislative Palace. The operation was completed in a matter of minutes. The Sandinistas took nearly one thousand hostages, including Somoza's nephew José Somoza Abrego and cousin Luis Pallais Debayle. After forty-eight hours of bargaining, Somoza was forced to accept another humiliating defeat. He agreed to release fifty-nine political prisoners and to pay the Sandinistas a $500,000 ransom. Another FSLN communiqué was broadcast on the state-controlled radio, this one calling for a general insurrection against the government. Once again, the prisoners, along with the guerrillas, were flown out of the country on a government jet, this time to Panama.

THE REVOLUTIONARY WAR

The success of Operation Pigpen spawned a countrywide uprising known as the September insurrection. Young people armed with pistols, hunting rifles, machetes, axes, homemade bombs, and even bottles and knives took over National Guard posts and police stations in nine major cities. Aware that they were fighting for their very existence, Somoza and the National Guard reacted with extreme intensity. In Managua, Matagalpa, Masaya, and León, they used tanks, helicopters, aerial strafing (firing machine guns from planes), and 50-caliber machine guns against rebels. In several cities, the military used white phosphorus bombs that incinerated people instantly and burned entire neighborhoods to the ground. At least thirty-five hundred peasants were killed, including large groups of innocent young men of fighting age who were slaughtered with machine guns.

Despite their tragic losses, Nicaraguans felt that Somoza would surely fall. He was no longer fighting isolated groups of guerrillas but an entire people. As one unnamed middle-class observer stated,

> *"I took part in student demonstrations and saw with horror fellow students being shot at by Somoza's National Guard."*[20]
>
> —Bianca Jagger, Nicaragua native and chair of the Bianca Jagger Human Rights Foundation, 2004

Local residents of Estelí, Nicaragua, pass by corpses in the street after a battle between the Sandinistas and National Guard in September 1978.

"With the September insurrection, thousands of us came to realize that in the FSLN we had both a military instrument capable of overthrowing the dictatorship, and a political organization whose program synthesized all the deeply felt history of the Nicaraguan people."

Somoza knew the end was near. He began selling off his illegally obtained assets and transferred millions of dollars to secret bank accounts overseas. U.S. politicians were beginning to realize that the Marxist Sandinistas might actually succeed. It was politically unacceptable to allow what was being called a second Cuba to be established in Nicaragua. In early 1979, Carter released $66 million in international aid to keep Somoza in power.

As the politicians made their bargains, FSLN leaders planned a massive final offensive against the National Guard. On May 29, 1979, coordinated assaults were launched against GN positions in several cities. Meanwhile, general strikes were called to coincide with the military attacks. This tactic allowed FSLN to take control of twenty-five towns and villages within weeks. By the middle of June, revolutionary juntas controlled half of Managua and all of León. By the end of the month, National Guard members were either quitting or defecting to the FSLN.

Victory!

Fifty-two days after it began, the insurrection was over. Somoza resigned on July 8, abandoning the battle-torn capital on July 17. He escaped

FSLN members and supporters celebrate their victory in Managua on July 20, 1979.

with about forty-five others in five private planes, landing at Homestead Air Force base near Miami, Florida. The next day, the National Guard dissolved. On July 19, the Sandinista revolution concluded as columns of fighters from across Nicaragua converged on the National Palace.

The red and black Sandinista flag was hoisted onto government buildings as well as the shacks and car antennas of average peasants. Thousands of liberated people fired their weapons in the air and blew off firecrackers. Church bells rang all day long.

The revolutionary war lasted about two years. But the people of Nicaragua had been fighting for their freedom since the 1920s, when Sandino first called them to arms. For the first time in history, the country was in the hands of laborers, students, farmers, and other downtrodden citizens. What they would accomplish in the aftermath of the revolution remained to be seen.

The Death of Anastasio Somoza

ANASTASIO SOMOZA FLED NICARAGUA on July 18, 1979, as Sandinista troops closed in on the Presidential Palace in Managua. Although he escaped to Miami, he was denied residence in the United States by President Jimmy Carter. The ex-dictator took refuge in the South American nation of Paraguay, but his enemies refused to let him live in peace. On September 17, 1980, a team of revolutionary commandos led by Argentine guerrilla Enrique Gorriarán Merlo ambushed Somoza as he was being driven through the Paraguayan capital city of Asunción. The rebels fired two shots from their bazookas. Both hit Somoza's car, killing him instantly.

CHAPTER 3

The Honeymoon

ON THE MORNING OF JULY 19, 1979, people turning on their radios in Managua knew immediately that the forty-two-year reign of the Somoza dynasty was over. Instead of censored news broadcasts and pro-government messages, listeners heard a new kind of propaganda. The main station had been renamed Radio Sandino, and it was playing Indian folk songs, martial music, the Sandinista national anthem, and victory slogans.

The radio also transmitted messages from Nicaragua's new ruling body, the Governing Junta of National Reconstruction. The members of the junta were Comandante Daniel Ortega for the FSLN; Moises Hassan from the National Patriotic Front; Sergio Ramírez Mercado, an author and member of El Grupo de los Doce; businessman Alfonso Robelo Callejas; and Violeta Barrios de Chamorro, widow of the murdered *La Prensa* editor. Robelo and Chamorro did not agree with Sandinista Marxist philosophy but had long opposed Somoza and had worked toward his ouster.

In the radio broadcasts, the junta asked the public to display discipline, order, and kindness toward the defeated enemy. Local FSLN neighborhood groups were asked to oversee tasks previously performed by government administrators. This included everything from picking up the garbage to putting out fires and taking away the dead still lying in the streets. These were the first days of the Sandinista government in Nicaragua and the aftermath of a historic revolution.

Without Somoza or the National Guard to run the country, the junta faced many difficult tasks. Recalling the vacuum left by the dictator's defeat, one member of the national legislature wrote, "We took out the heart and the body fell. Now we must fill the empty space." The reality of the situation quickly ended the euphoria of victory for the comandantes of the revolution. The Sandinistas were now in control of a country that was in ruins. More than six hundred thousand people were homeless while the nation's roads, sewers, electric grid, and public buildings were devastated. What wasn't still in ruins from the 1972

THE GOVERNING JUNTA OF THE NATIONAL RECONSTRUCTION INCLUDED *(LEFT TO RIGHT)* SERGIO RAMÍREZ, DANIEL ORTEGA, VIOLETA BARRIOS DE CHAMORRO, ALFONSO ROBELO CALLEJAS, AND MOISES HASSAN.

earthquake had been destroyed during the years of the revolution.

It wasn't all bad news for the Sandinistas, however. A majority of Nicaraguans believed in the Sandinista programs, and people were joyous Somoza had been deposed. Their gratitude and support proved to be very important in the years that followed.

The Sandinista Directorate

In the early days of Sandinista power, average Nicaraguans were willing to give the government leeway to try new programs. For this reason, the early period is known as the revolutionary honeymoon. During this phase, the comandantes of the revolution appointed a diverse group of men and women to take over important cabinet positions. Humberto Ortega became minister of defense, while Borge took over as minister of the interior. In this job, Borge would supervise the national police force, state security, and Nicaragua's notoriously violent prisons. His new role was somewhat ironic—as historian and *New York Times* reporter Stephen Kinzer wrote, "[Borge] had spent most of his life hiding from the law, and now, in one of those turnabouts that are the essence of revolution, he took control of the country's police apparatus." One of Borge's first duties was to round up thousands of National Guardsmen. These men were considered criminals and counterrevolutionaries, and the Sandinistas planned to put them on trial and jail them.

After several weeks, the governing junta renamed the governing body the National Directorate, or DN. This group held absolute power, and its members were not democratically elected. They had no intention of sharing power with anyone outside the FSLN.

Rounding Up the National Guard

AFTER CLAIMING VICTORY, THE Sandinistas immediately outlawed torture and abolished the death penalty. However, they dealt with former members of the National Guard in a harsh manner. Sandinista police officials rounded up nearly every member of the ten-thousand-man Guard, most of whom had surrendered voluntarily. While former guardsmen believed they would not be punished, Sandinistas viewed them as criminals who would likely take part in a counterrevolution.

To deal with the volatile situation, the Sandinistas created an official tribunal. After perfunctory trials, prison wardens and officers who had ordered cities bombed were given thirty-year prison sentences. Low-level officials and young men who served in the infantry were charged with what was called illicit association and membership in a criminal organization. These guardsmen were given quick trials and handed ten-year sentences, although they were not presented with specific evidence of crimes committed. Some opposition leaders decried the nature of the tribunals since the outcome was predetermined and the soldiers were not allowed to present a defense. However, the opposition protests were largely ignored.

But the Sandinistas had been planning for the post-revolutionary period for many years, and the FSLN quickly implemented their fifteen-point Immediate Program, issued in 1978. The government planned to improve conditions for workers; build houses, schools, and hospitals; and institute land reform so peasants could farm for themselves.

Whatever the idealistic plans for the future, the first order of business was to reconstruct the national economy. The Sandinistas themselves would soon be overthrown if they failed to provide jobs, export crops, and provide food for the masses.

To feed people and provide employment for farmers, the Sandinistas immediately confiscated all Somoza's properties, as well as those of his friends. Within weeks the Sandinistas had turned over 20 percent of all agricultural lands in the country to the Nicaraguan people. The government also seized a large number of industrial and commercial properties to put people back to work. To direct money toward large public projects, the Sandinistas nationalized (put under government control) the bank system. By controlling the banks, the government could lend money to peasants for planting crops. They could also make grants to village governments so they could build schools and health clinics.

Most of the Sandinista actions followed Marxist ideology to return the means of production to the people. But the new government was practical too. Although they were under no obligation to do so, the Sandinistas continued to pay off multibillion-dollar foreign debts incurred by Somoza over the years, including money borrowed from international bankers to fight the Sandinistas. The Sandinistas paid these loans in order to maintain friendly relations with Western banks. After setting up a payment plan, the new government made every interest payment on time between 1980 and 1982.

A Rocky Honeymoon

To give people a voice in their government, the Sandinistas created a legislative body called the Council of State. This council had forty-seven members from nearly every political party and organization in Nicaragua, including Communists and former members of Somoza's Liberal Party. The group was organized to create a balance of power.

> *"[We took power] with great enthusiasm and a great desire to transform the country, but also with the worry that we would have to confront the United States."*
>
> —Daniel Ortega, leader of the Sandinista Liberation Front, 1998

It was meant to keep the governing junta in check until elections could be held in 1985. Sandinistas held a large majority on the Council of State, which diluted the votes of the other parties. Nonetheless, non-Sandinistas, known as the patriotic opposition, chose to work within the system to achieve their goals.

On the far left of the patriotic opposition, the Marxist-Leninist Popular Action Movement and the Revolutionary Worker's Party wanted to nationalize all property, exclude all rightists from the government, and create a dictatorship based on the Soviet Union. To the right of the FSLN, groups such as the Patriotic Front and the Popular Social Christian Party supported limited government but were willing to tolerate Sandinista programs. Whether left or right, all members were strongly opposed to U.S. intervention in their country.

Aid from Cuba

When the Sandinistas nationalized the banks and seized many businesses, there was widespread alarm in the United States. Tensions were further inflamed when Nicaragua reversed Somoza's long-standing policies and established diplomatic ties to Cuba. Kinzer explains why the Sandinistas looked to Cuba's president Fidel Castro for aid:

> Few Sandinista comandantes had ever lived normal lives, much less faced the complexities of public administration, so it was not surprising that they looked for foreign help. Because they deeply mistrusted the United States for its historical sins, there was no possibility of inviting American advisors into the highest councils of their government. Cuba was at the other extreme, the most trustworthy and fraternal of nations. Cuban and Nicaraguan revolutionaries considered themselves the same flesh, and Cuba most closely approximated the country the Sandinistas sought to build. The Sandinistas understood the need to adjust their tactics to Nicaraguan realities, but their ultimate goal—as it had been for nearly two decades—was to make Nicaragua the second revolutionary Marxist state in the Americas.

Cuba responded by providing millions of dollars in reconstruction aid to Nicaragua. The Managua airport served as the center of this relief effort. Cuban airliners filled with desperately needed supplies landed every day. Cuba also sent hundreds of experienced medical personnel and government advisers.

Some Cuban imports caused great distress in the United States and in neighboring countries. Shiploads of weapons began pouring in from Cuba and other Communist nations including North Korea, the Soviet Union, and Czechoslovakia. Cuban military leaders also traveled to Nicaragua to help Humberto Ortega create a strong Sandinista army. Several Cuban military experts even became Nicaraguan citizens so they could take top roles in the national military and security agencies.

The Literacy Crusade

The majority of Cubans traveling to Nicaragua were not military advisers. They were top Cuban education officials accompanied by thousands of schoolteachers. These visitors took a lead role in reorganizing Nicaragua's educational system.

Under Somoza, Nicaragua's schools were among the worst in Latin America. The government spent little money on education because wealthy leading citizens wanted uneducated young people who would work in fields and factories. By the late seventies, only 65 percent of Nicaragua's children attended school. Of those, less than a quarter graduated from sixth grade. Most rural schools offered only one or two years of classes, and three-quarters of the rural population was illiterate. Even those interested in education could not enroll in secondary schools since these were expensive, private institutions. Few Nicaraguans attended college, and most of the rich sent their children to universities in the United States.

As promised during the revolution, the Sandinistas started a crash course called the Literacy Crusade to teach citizens to read and write. Cuban teachers flooded the countryside, joined by one hundred thousand Nicaraguan volunteer teachers. Schools were set up in storefronts, churches, and other available buildings. They held classes about twelve hours a week, which was a major commitment for most workers who attended. Humanitarian aid workers Frances Moore Lappé and Joseph Collins observed, "We found it astonishing that so many poor peasants, whose lives are already physically exhausting, would voluntarily add twelve hours of mentally exhausting work to their week."

Despite the extra burden, half a million people gained rudimentary reading skills by early 1980. Nicaragua's national illiteracy rate dropped dramatically from more than 50 percent to 13 percent of the population. The United Nations Educational, Scientific and Cultural Organization (UNESCO) recognized the great success of the literacy campaign with the award called the Nadezhda Krupskaya International Prize.

In addition to the literacy campaign, the Sandinista Ministry of Education (MED) set up preschools, technical schools, and adult education programs. Within two years, the MED oversaw the

VILLAGERS ATTEND CLASSES AS PART OF THE LITERACY CRUSADE IN NICARAGUA IN THE 1980S.

Teaching People to Read and Write

MUCH OF NICARAGUA'S LITERACY campaign was run from adult education centers located in storefront offices piled high with books and notebooks. Three unnamed volunteer teachers in Santa Maria describe their work:

> There are two centers in Santa Maria, 23 in the whole municipality. In our area, 800 people entered the literacy program and more than half finished. We now [in 1981] have 331 in our center. Some have just learned to read and write; others knew how but never had had any real schooling.
>
> We try to get people interested by telling them that if they can't read, they won't know what's going on. They won't be able to participate fully in all the changes. And we tell them that we'll give them lots of free materials to help them—books, pencils and paper.

construction of 739 new schools. Most of them were in rural areas that had never had schools before. Some people criticized the Sandinista literacy programs, however. Most textbooks were political, and teachers were required to teach Sandinista political beliefs.

"We Can Produce with the Help of the Government"

The focus on education was second only to agricultural reform. Farm programs were seen as a way to win peasants over to the Sandinista cause and quiet any opposition. Before the revolution, only a few thousand wealthy families controlled most of Nicaragua's farmland. This forced most peasants to work on plantations for extremely low wages. In the weeks after Somoza's government fell, this policy was quickly reversed. As rich landowners fled the countryside, their huge farmhouses, called haciendas, were taken over by peasants. In Managua the government decreed that eventually all such lands would be converted into state-owned collective farms.

Many landowners strongly resisted the Sandinista land reform program. Although some had been wealthy Somoza supporters, most were simply middle-class farmers. Coffee grower Ernesto Reyes describes how his land was confiscated:

THESE WORKERS ARE HARVESTING TOBACCO ON A COLLECTIVE FARM IN NICARAGUA IN 1983. THE SANDINISTA GOVERNMENT TURNED FARMLAND INTO STATE-OWNED COLLECTIVE FARMS.

When [the Sandinistas] saw that we had money, they became our enemies. They kicked us off our farm, out of our house by force. They manhandled us with weapons. . . . Everyone who had a little bit of money to live more or less comfortably, [the government] robbed. It wasn't only us that they robbed; because if they had only stolen from us maybe we would have asked why. But it wasn't only us, it was everyone, and we had to fight back.

"All those who didn't agree with the Sandinista policies were subjected to confiscations and imprisonment, and their lives were threatened."

—Oscar Manuel Sobalvarro, Sandinista resister, 1998

Reyes and others like him were unemployed and landless. They banded together to form the Anti-Sandinista Popular Militias (MILPAs).

The unfairness of the land reform policies caused tensions to flare. But there is little doubt that the nationalization of farms profoundly changed Nicaragua. About 28 percent of all land under cultivation was nationalized, and about 60 percent of all peasants in the country received some land. Peasant cooperatives made up of several dozen members used small government loans to buy seeds and machinery to farm these lands. Commenting on the success of one such cooperative in Estelí, farmer Mercedes Arce Torruño described his experience in 1980.

> I grew up here. . . . I worked here, on this land, since I was eight years old. They used to pay me only [about a dollar] a day. [Before the revolution, the owners] said we couldn't make it. The rich people said we didn't have enough knowledge. They said we'd never be able to work together. But we've done it! We've shown them that what they said about us were lies. We've shown we can produce with the help of the government.

Grassroots Groups

Peasant farmers like Torruño were members of various OPs formed during the early days of the revolution. After the Sandinista victory, these same grassroots organizations helped solve problems that members faced and, in this way, helped foster a sense of community. Sociologist Luis Hector Serra writes that the actions of the grassroots groups "contributed to an improvement in the living conditions of the lower classes and at the same time, created an understanding of participation and organization necessary to build a democratic system." And through the OPs, Nicaraguans learned the value of freedom of expression, which they had been denied for decades under Somoza.

In the earliest days of Sandinista rule, OPs took over important government functions. For example, in urban areas, the Sandinista Defense Committees (CDS) acted as an informal police organization to prevent looting and anarchy. Urban CDS also coordinated dozens of neighborhood programs through elected leaders. In Managua about 550 block captains attended regular meetings where they dealt with many issues. They planned Saturday night dances, arranged book collections for a new library, and managed food distribution. Block captains also debated ways to improve mass transit and discussed renaming streets for martyrs of the revolution. Government officials sometimes attended the meetings, answered questions, and discussed public policy.

Providing Food and Medicine

In the countryside, an OP called the Rural Workers Association, or ATC, took control of many ranches and haciendas. The group also formed rural farming cooperatives and coordinated labor on farms. Another important group, the National Union of Ranchers and Farmers (UNAG), was made up of owners of small- and medium-sized farms. Members met with the Council of State to institute agricultural reforms that would benefit them. UNAG was also instrumental in setting up small stores in factories and workplaces to sell meat and other farm products produced by members. These outlets, called peasant stores, were located throughout Nicaragua and provided inexpensive food for workers and peasants.

One of the most significant OPs, called the Popular Health Workdays, was dedicated to public hygiene and the prevention of disease. Its thirty-six thousand members worked with the Ministry of Health (MINSA) to reduce incidents of malaria, polio, and other deadly diseases. In addition to distributing vaccines and medicine, the OP worked closely with other grassroots groups that cleaned up roadside sewage, provided potable water, and maintained clean irrigation canals to prevent the spread of disease.

The Popular Health Workdays also worked with MINSA to run the National Unified Health System. This program brought together Nicaragua's public and private hospitals and health-care workers to provide health care for all citizens.

WOMEN'S RIGHTS

Many of the improvements instituted by the Sandinistas were beneficial to women. In a nation where the average twenty-four-year-old woman had four or five children, food, education, and medicine were primary concerns. But the Sandinistas also promised to improve the social standing of women. Even from its earliest days, the FSLN called for the end of gender discrimination and for political and economic equality for all women. By the end of the revolution, one-third of all Sandinista officials were women.

Women's issues were the focus of one of Nicaragua's largest grassroots groups, the Luisa Amanda Espinoza Association of Nicaraguan Women (AMNLAE), named for the first FSLN woman to die in battle. The AMNLAE has been credited for supporting many gains in Nicaraguan women's rights. Chapters invited women from all levels of Nicaraguan society to learn more about the women's liberation movement, reproductive rights, and ways to obtain equal rights through changes in politics and law.

Women also took leading roles in many local CDs and labor organizations. Despite their gains, however, male party leaders often con-

Luisa Amanda Espinoza

LUISA AMANDA ESPINOZA WAS the first FSLN woman to die in battle. Somoza's agents murdered her in 1970 when she was twenty-one for allowing her home in León to be used as a safe house for Sandinistas hiding from government officials. In 1980 the Luisa Amanda Espinoza Association of Nicaraguan Women was named for her.

sidered women's issues to be of lesser concern. In addition, Nicaraguan women remained almost totally responsible for child rearing and housekeeping. Women also had to work, often more than ten hours a day. This left most with little time for political participation. Nonetheless, the AMNLAE grew to include eighty-five thousand members, and many provided support for the Sandinista cause. They sewed backpacks and uniforms, raised money for community projects, and helped the families of the forty thousand soldiers wounded in the revolution. AMNLAE members also set up reading rooms and ran day care centers.

The move toward women's equality in Nicaragua paralleled the women's liberation movement in the United States and elsewhere in the early 1980s. However, the AMNLAE remained under the control of the male-dominated FSLN, and traditional Latin American gender roles proved difficult to change, and the success of the Nicaraguan women's movement was mixed. As Margaret Randall, an expert in Nicaraguan women's issues, writes in *Sandino's Daughter Revisited*:

> The Sandinista revolution brought young women, with their Spanish Catholic heritage of chastity and submission, out into an arena of public struggle. A decade of revolutionary government promoted women's rights in health, education, labor, leadership, and more egalitarian legislation—some of it successful, some not.

During those early days of Sandinista rule, women's issues were only part of a complex plan to remake Nicaraguan society. After centuries of repression, women, farmers, workers, and students were all bursting with optimism and fresh ideas.

A Woman Leader's Perspective

DORA MARIA TÉLLEZ PLAYED an extraordinary role in the Sandinista revolution. In 1978, at the age of twenty-three, she participated in Operation Pigpen. After national liberation, she became the minister of public health and was vice president of the Council of State. Téllez described her life as a government official in the immediate aftermath of the revolution:

> [Most] of us in that early leadership of the Managua committee were women. . . . Our ways of seeing things were sometimes in conflict [with men], and that caused problems. But what was I doing during this period? Mostly I spent my time in the factories, among the workers—and in the neighborhoods. Talking to people, day after day. There were so many problems to be solved, everywhere you went. There were workers running factories on their own because the owners were Somoza people and they'd left the country. Labor relations were changing so fast you could hardly keep up with them. Workers were beginning to organize en masse: some into neighborhood block committees, others in the unions. . . .
>
> That was a very special time, because everyone was organizing, mobilizing; they were willing to listen to what you had to say, and they'd speak their own minds, too. I remember they'd invite me to give political talks, to explain our political project. And people would ask thousands of questions. . . . In Nicaragua, neither

Somoza nor the Conservatives had ever offered a political project that integrated anyone: they never even dialogued with people; they never explained who they were or what they wanted.

But ours was an integrated project that included everyone who wanted to take part. It made people subjects—instead of objects—of their own history. It was like a huge wave, something new; and people got enthusiastic, excited. . . . And those years were among the richest of my life.

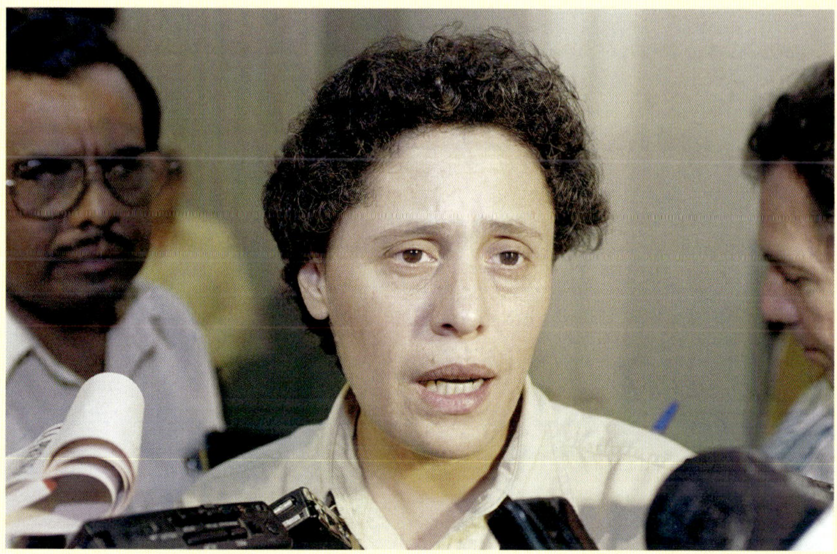

Dora Maria Téllez speaks to reporters in 1995. Téllez held important roles in the Sandinista government in the 1970s and 1980s.

CHAPTER 4

Low-Intensity Conflict

WITH SOMOZA GONE and the National Guard in ruins, the Sandinistas had a unique opportunity to put their programs in place. But many Nicaraguans whose lands and businesses were nationalized by the Sandinistas were violently opposed to the regime. And the Sandinistas failed to consider how their Marxist victory worried politicians who lived thousands of miles to the north in the United States.

In the United States, President Jimmy Carter had been horrified by Somoza's human rights record. But he was not ready to surrender U.S. influence in the region to a Marxist regime. In 1979 U.S. national security adviser Zbigniew Brzezinski advised Carter not to support the Sandinistas, saying, "We have to demonstrate that we are still the decisive force in determining the political outcomes in Central America and that we will not permit others [such as Cuba and the Soviet Union] to intervene."

In order to apply U.S. force in the aftermath of the revolution, Carter supported plans by the U.S. military to resurrect the National Guard. This would balance the power of the Sandinista People's Army (EPS), the only organized military force operating in Nicaragua. When this effort failed, Carter promised economic aid in return for Sandinista cooperation with U.S. goals in the region. One month after the revolution ended, Carter loaned the new government $15 million in emergency relief aid so the Sandinistas could begin to repair the housing and infrastructure destroyed during the war. Then, in September 1979, Carter pushed legislation through Congress authorizing a $75 million assistance package to the Sandinistas.

After the aid bill was passed, FSLN commanders were invited to the White House. This was part of Carter's strategy to moderate Sandinista Marxism through friendship, negotiation, and aid. Viron P. Vaky, the assistant secretary of state for inter-American affairs told the president, "The [aftermath] of the Nicaraguan revolution will . . . [depend] on how the U.S. perceives it and relates to it. . . . We might write it off as already radicalized and beyond redemption, but that would surely drive the revolution into deeper radicalization."

While Carter was concerned with events in Central America, he had much more urgent problems in the oil-rich nation of Iran. A violent uprising led by fundamentalist leader Ayatollah Ruhollah Khomeini had deposed the U.S.-backed shah of Iran, Mohammad Reza Pahlavi. In October 1979, young supporters of Khomeini invaded the U.S. Embassy and took fifty-two Americans as hostages. After a mission to rescue the hostages failed disastrously, Carter's popularity plummeted.

The Iran Hostage Crisis

IN 1979 PRESIDENT JIMMY Carter's most pressing problem was not the Sandinista revolution but the Iranian hostage crisis. Problems began in February 1979, several months before the end of the Sandinista revolution, when Islamic religious leader Ayatollah Ruhollah Khomeini deposed Shah Mohammad Reza Pahlavi. Like Somoza, the shah was a repressive dictator supported by the United States for decades, who tortured and killed opponents. After Khomeini's followers kidnapped fifty-two Americans as hostages from the U.S. Embassy in Tehran, the capital of Iran, public opinion in the United States turned against Carter. His approval ratings continued to fall as radical Islamists paraded blindfolded Americans before television cameras day after day. An unsuccessful hostage rescue attempt by U.S. Army Rangers in April 1980 caused further outrage in the United States. Carter's declining popularity led to Ronald Reagan's success in the presidential election that November.

The Honeymoon Is Over

As events unfolded in Iran, the Sandinista government was having its own problems. Trouble began when the FSLN added eleven more members to the thirty-three-member Council of State. This gave the Sandinistas majority control of the council and significantly reduced the power of the non-Marxists. Two members, Violeta Chamorro and Alfonso Robelo, quit the council, with Chamorro noting, "The FSLN has violated its trust and broken the political unity of Nicaragua."

Chamorro's views were expressed in *La Prensa*, which was openly critical of the Sandinistas. The newspaper featured stories about the disappearance or mistreatment of people by the police. There were also reports that questioned the strong-arm tactics the Sandinistas used to take over some plantations. These articles created great anxiety among the middle and upper classes in Nicaragua. Fearing that their country would turn into a totalitarian regime, many fled to Miami. They shut down their businesses and took badly needed money out of the country.

Unhappy with the bad publicity, the Sandinistas shut down *La Prensa* for a time. This led to charges of censorship and calls for freedom of the press. Bayardo Arce, former journalism professor and member of the directorate, responded, "We support freedom of the press, but, of course, the freedom of the press we support [is] freedom of the press that supports the revolution." Arce was forced to back down, however, under pressure from the public. The paper was allowed to reopen, but the Sandinista government established its own newspaper *Nuevo Diario* to publicize the FSLN party line.

By August 1980, the issue of voting further splintered Nicaraguan unity. Opposition business leaders from the Superior Council of Private Enterprises (COSEP) demanded that the Sandinistas set a date for democratic elections. After first agreeing to hold elections in 1981, the Sandinistas announced they would not do so until 1985. It also prohibited political campaigning until 1984. This was justified by the excuse that Nicaraguans needed to rebuild the country before holding elections.

The FSLN declared that it alone was the sole guardian of the peoples' interests. Ortega, speaking about the decree to a group of enthusiastic young supporters, said.

> As you can all understand, the elections of which we are talking are very distinct from the elections that are wanted by the oligarchs [wealthy people] and traitors, Conservatives and

> Liberals, the reactionaries and imperialists. . . . Keep in mind that [ours] are elections to advance revolutionary power, not to raffle off power, because the people [already] have power through . . . the Sandinista Front of National Liberation and its National Directorate. . . . This is Sandinista Democracy.

Counterrevolutionaries

Ortega's announcement outraged many. Members of the opposition were hoping for elections to moderate the more radical elements of the regime. One of those angered by Ortega's announcement was Jorge Salazar, a forty-one-year-old coffee plantation owner. As president of the Union of Nicaraguan Agricultural Producers (UPANIC), Salazar was very influential among Nicaragua's private farmers.

The Sandinistas had appointed Salazar to the Council of State in May 1980. But he was holding clandestine meetings with discontented Sandinista military officials. Some of these officials were former members of the National Guard, and they were ready to start an uprising. These early counterrevolutionaries looked to Salazar as a powerful figure who could lead their new government. Salazar incited his own supporters to violence by stating that the only way the Sandinistas could be removed from power was to "shoot them out."

Salazar formed a plan in which several Sandinista army officers would stage a coup (overthrow of the government). The officers would arrest members of the Sandinista Directorate and seize the radio and television stations to announce a change of power. Working toward that goal, Salazar distributed weapons among the coffee growers in UPANIC. The plot was discovered in November 1980, however, and Salazar was assassinated as he got out of his car at a gas station, most likely by Sandinista soldiers.

Allegedly, soldiers planted several M16 rifles in the trunk of Salazar's car after shooting him. This was meant to implicate him in the counter-revolutionary movement. Opposition members saw Salazar's murder as a sign that the Sandinistas were willing to assassinate people deemed a threat to their power, since they eliminated the legal death penalty.

The Reagan Doctrine

While the bloody events unfolded in Managua, few Americans were aware of the situation in Nicaragua, which was rarely in the U.S. news. The Iranian hostage crisis was making headlines every day, however, and Americans were faced with other related problems, such as skyrocketing gas prices, 11 percent unemployment, and crippling inflation. When conservative Republican Ronald Reagan ran against Carter in November 1980, he won by a landslide. Republicans gained a majority of Senate seats for the first time since 1952.

Reagan was a staunch anti-communist who was convinced that Soviet power was a serious threat to the United States. His political opponents accused him of exaggerating the danger, but many

"We must stand by all our democratic allies. And we must not break faith with those who are risking their lives—on every continent, from Afghanistan to Nicaragua—to defy Soviet-supported aggression and secure rights which have been ours from birth."

—anti-communist Reagan Doctrine, 1985

Americans supported this belief. And in the early 1980s, Reagan's unwavering opposition to Marxist or Communist regimes throughout the developing world boosted his popularity.

From his first days in office, the president formulated policies based on his extreme hatred of Communism. These principles came to be known as the Reagan Doctrine. Robert McFarlane, the president's national security adviser, explained the thinking behind the Reagan Doctrine:

> We had just witnessed a five-year period where the Soviet Union tried out a stratagem of sponsoring guerrilla movements that would topple moderate regimes, and install their own totalitarian successor, and they had phenomenal success . . . in Angola, Ethiopia . . . Afghanistan, Mozambique, [and] Nicaragua.

Many would disagree with McFarlane's reference to Somoza as moderate and the Sandinistas as totalitarian. However, people in the Reagan administration deliberately used inflammatory terms to describe the situation in Nicaragua. This was done to prepare Americans for a violent offensive against the Sandinistas. McFarlane continued, "If we could not muster an effective counter to Cuban-Sandinista strategy in our own backyard, it was far less likely we could do so in the years ahead in more distant locations. . . . We had to win this one."

Reagan was facing another looming problem in the region. During his first days in office, a civil war broke out in El Salvador, a small Central American nation about the size of Massachusetts. As in Nicaragua, a repressive, U.S.-backed right-wing regime was fighting a group of leftist and Communist guerrillas. The rebels called themselves the Farabundo Martí National Liberation Front (FMLN). It

The El Salvador Connection

IN THE LATE 1970s, guerrilla fighters from neighboring El Salvador fought with the Sandinistas during the revolution. After the victory, Sandinistas returned the favor when a similar rebellion was unfolding in El Salvador. After Reagan was elected president in 1980, many believed he might send U.S. troops to fight the Central American revolutionaries. The Sandinistas thought it was in their best interest to keep their neighboring rebels well armed. By the end of 1981, according to the U.S. State Department, Nicaragua was also providing the Salvadorans with training, command-and-control headquarters, and other vital supplies.

While it was clear that the Nicaraguans were helping the Salvadoran guerrillas, few foreign-policy experts could find a connection between the rebels in El Salvador and the Soviet Union. However, Reagan described the insurgents as Soviet-backed terrorists. And he accused the Sandinistas of supporting terrorism with their weapons shipments to the guerrillas. Therefore, Reagan was able to direct the Central Intelligence Agency (CIA) to help overthrow the Sandinista government for supposedly helping a Soviet-backed revolution in Central America.

was feared that El Salvador could fall by the end of 1981. The revolution might then spread to neighboring Guatemala.

Low-Intensity Conflict

Polls taken in early 1980 showed that Americans felt "humiliated" by the Iranians and "out-gunned by the Russians."[40] However, many people were also suffering from what was called the Vietnam Syndrome. In the aftermath of U.S. involvement in the war in Vietnam (1957–1975), there was widespread resistance to sending young U.S. soldiers to fight and risk their lives in distant third world conflicts.

Reagan understood that a military invasion of Nicaragua would be extremely unpopular both at home and internationally. Therefore, his advisers formulated an alternative strategy called low-intensity conflict (LIC) to deal with the Sandinistas.

Low-intensity conflict is unlike a formal military operation in which U.S. forces fight other uniformed soldiers. Instead, LIC consists of methods meant to subvert and destroy an enemy government. In Nicaragua these operations would include economic disruption, sabotage, and political assassination meant to destabilize the regime.

Reagan planned to wage the LIC as a covert, or secret, war. Former National Guard members and other opponents of the Sandinistas would be provided with training, arms, money, and intelligence from the United States. According to one unnamed proponent of LIC, the United States would engage in "total war at the grassroots level . . . without the domestic and international political backlash that a conventional war would provoke."

The low-intensity conflict planned for Nicaragua proceeded on various fronts. The first centered on paramilitary operations, in which civilian fighters, many of whom were former National Guard members, were trained to carry out bloody attacks using military weapons and tactics. These paramilitary forces were trained by the Central

"Low-intensity conflict is like a deadly bomb wrapped with beautiful paper. It couples the use of explicit terror with rhetoric about 'freedom,' 'democracy,' and 'national interest.'"

—Jack Nelson-Pallmeyer, U.S. religious scholar and former Central America resident, 1990

Intelligence Agency (CIA) to assassinate judges, police, and state security officials. They also would attack state-owned cooperatives and health clinics in the countryside to punish peasants for supporting the Sandinistas. Economic targets would include oil pipelines; port facilities; radio, telephone, and television centers; and military depots. Weapons were supplied by the U.S. Department of Defense, which acted under orders to provide maximum support to the paramilitary operations. In one program, known as Operation Kettle Tipped, the Pentagon obtained weapons captured by Israelis in Lebanon and shipped them to the Nicaraguan counterrevolutionaries.

Another aspect of the LIC plan for Nicaragua centered on destroying the already weak Nicaraguan economy by denying aid. Officials refused to make aid payments promised by Carter. They also rescinded loans to Nicaragua that had previously been approved from the World Bank or the Inter-American Development Bank. In addition, the Reagan administration applied pressure on European and Central American nations to cut aid, reduce trade, and isolate the Sandinistas from the international community. The Reagan administration hoped that the resulting economic distress would incite Nicaraguans to back counterrevolutionary forces and overthrow the Sandinistas.

Recruiting a Force

The United States initiated the low-intensity conflict against Nicaragua less than two months after Reagan's inauguration. To build public support, Reagan gave speeches warning that the Sandinistas were shipping Cuban-supplied arms to the rebels in El Salvador. On March 9, 1981, Reagan signed an executive order to provide $19.5 million for CIA operations in the region. Weeks later, the administration acted to deny Nicaragua trade credits. These credits had allowed Nicaraguan farmers and factory owners to import desperately needed supplies from the United States.

In late September 1981, the United States stepped up pressure on Nicaragua. Reagan announced that the Pentagon would conduct a joint military operation, called Halcón Vista (Hawk's View), on the Atlantic coast of Honduras, on October 7 to 9. This caused rumors to circulate that the United States was preparing to invade Nicaragua.

On November 17, Reagan formally began the CIA covert war by signing National Security Decision Directive (NSDD) 17. The top-secret directive gave the CIA another $19.9 million and the power to recruit a five-hundred-man force of anti-Sandinista fighters. Upon signing the NSDD, Reagan stated that fighting the Sandinistas was "important to the national security of the United States."

In the weeks that followed, CIA operatives expanded contacts with former National Guard officers and organized several small opposition groups. These were formed into a proxy, or paramilitary army, called the Nicaraguan Democratic Force (FDN). This force based its operations in Honduras, which formed the northern front of the war. The FDN forces were called counterrevolutionaries by the Sandinistas, or *contrarevolucionarios* in Spanish. This was abbreviated to Contras, a label the anti-Marxist forces chose to embrace. Commander Enrique Bermúdez was put in charge of the FDN. This was a controversial move. Bermúdez was a former military attaché, or diplomatic representative, to the United States for the Somoza government.

Most of the money the United States directed toward the Contras was funneled through the FDN. However, according to Robert Owen, one of the Reagan administration's liaisons with the Contras, members of the FDN were "liars [motivated] by greed and power." This presented an image problem for the CIA, who did not want the operation run solely by former Somoza backers. To balance the power, the CIA recruited a populist leader, Edén Pastora, Commander Zero, who had led the Sandinista assault on Somoza's National Congress.

Pastora had become disenchanted with the Sandinistas when most of the leaders moved into Managua's luxury residences after the revolution. He thought they were more concerned with propaganda and ideology than helping the nation's poor. Even before Reagan was elected, Pastora formed the Democratic Revolutionary Alliance (ARDE) in Costa Rica with Robelo, a former member of the Governing Junta. ARDE received a major boost from the CIA in 1982. The United States began giving Pastora about a million dollars every

FDN commander Enrique Bermúdez stands in front of Contra troops at a training camp in the mid-1980s. Bermúdez was put in charge of FDN troops in 1981.

Sandinista troops patrol the Nicaraguan border with Honduras in 1982. The United States funded training facilities and military bases near the border in Honduras for the Contras.

month to act as the southern front against the Sandinistas operating out of Costa Rica.

The United States went on to secure pledges from Honduran officials to allow the Contras to train in their country and began a program to train one thousand additional rebels in Argentina. Millions of dollars were funneled into Honduras for the construction of training facilities and military bases near the Nicaraguan border. Security Directive 17 also contained a controversial provision that allowed the CIA to use money and equipment provided by foreign governments for the covert war in Nicaragua. This meant that dozens of nations, including antidemocratic regimes in Saudi Arabia and South Africa, secretly provided monetary and military support for the conflict.

A State of Emergency

With CIA money, machine guns, trucks, and artillery, the Contras began a series of minor attacks on Nicaraguan targets. The Sandinistas calculated that the best way to resist the Contras was to rally support from the people. To do so, the FSLN organized rallies where officials gave speeches that strongly condemned Reagan and the imperialist actions of the United States.

Ortega also moved to shore up Sandinista power by declaring a state of economic and social emergency on September 9, 1981. The initiative was meant to notify Nicaraguans that their country was under attack and that they needed to unite against the enemy. On October 3, Defense Minister Humberto Ortega instituted a plan that coordinated a series of political rallies and rowdy demonstrations across the nation. The pro-Sandinista magazine *Envío* described measures taken during the anti-interventionist campaign:

> Often there were discussions in classrooms, factories and markets before the demonstrations. The people participated with excitement and enthusiasm. The discussions and demonstrations did not unfold in an atmosphere of anger or aggression, but rather one of unity and determination. Those participating [said] they will not easily lose what has cost them so much to obtain. The demonstrations themselves had an educational aspect. The leaders explained the principal problems facing Nicaragua, the economic emergency, the aggressive policies

Armed Attacks

"ACCORDING TO NICARAGUAN OFFICIALS, since May 1 [1982] there have been over 50 armed attacks in Nicaragua and at least 100 Nicaraguan military and civilian deaths. These attacks are no longer perpetrated by small, ill-equipped bands, according to the Nicaraguan military, but rather by counterrevolutionary military units, well-equipped with sophisticated weapons and logistical and communications capacity.

"The most barbarous of the attacks took place on July 24 when 100 counterrevolutionaries crossed from Honduras and attacked the town of San Francisco del Norte, 12 km [8 miles]. from the border. There is no army unit there and the town was defended by some 30-40 civilian militia. Fifteen of these townspeople were killed, and 8 of them severely tortured and their bodies mutilated. Eight others were kidnapped and taken to Honduras. The invading group painted the letters FDN (Nicaraguan Democratic Front) on the walls of many houses. They painted many slogans such as "With God and Patriotism we will drive out communism." According to the testimony of townspeople, the attackers tried to force one man, whom they tortured to death, to repeat slogans against the government."
—*Envío* magazine, August 1982

of the Reagan administration and the delicate and critical world situation. This dialogue was one of the most significant aspects of the mobilizations. . . . Slogans generated during the mobilizations expressed the strong anti-imperialistic and anti-interventionist, but not anti-American, sentiments of the crowds.

Massive mobilizations and educational actions did little to deter the Contras. Between March 14 and June 21, 1982, the counterrevolutionaries carried out at least one hundred operations. The Contras burned warehouses and food crops, sabotaged bridges, and directed sniper fire at small Sandinista military patrols. According to the U.S. Defense Intelligence Agency (DIA), the Contras also assassinated minor government officials. In the months that followed, the attacks on civilians and nonmilitary targets increased dramatically. Nicaragua was at war, and the low-intensity conflict would affect everyone in the country.

CHAPTER 5

The Counterrevolution

RONALD REAGAN'S DECISION TO AID the Nicaraguan Contras through the CIA was supposed to be top secret. The president denied the United States was involved with the guerrilla operations in Nicaragua. However, in March 1982, the National Security Decision Directive was leaked to the press, and reports about it were featured in newspapers across the country.

The Reagan administration downplayed the significance of the aid. The president claimed Americans were not supporting former Somoza allies but moderates who opposed the Sandinistas. Admiral Bobby Ray Inman, deputy director of the CIA, noted that the $19 million authorized by the directive was not much money to wage a war: "Nineteen million or $29 million isn't going to buy you much of any kind [of war] these days, and certainly not against that kind of military force [fielded by the Sandinistas]."

Although the administration downplayed the Contra aid, congressional opposition to Reagan's Nicaragua policy grew. When CIA director William Casey appeared before a House of Representatives subcommittee in 1983, he was asked tough questions. Representatives were concerned about attacks on innocent civilians. They wanted to know how the United States could control the Contras once they gained power so that Nicaragua would not be taken over by another brutal dictator like Somoza. They also feared that the combat could spread beyond Nicaragua's borders, inciting a major war between several countries in the region.

Freedom Fighters

To counter congressional opposition—and gain support from the American people—the Reagan administration attempted to change public perceptions of the operation. To do so, the president enlisted military psychological operations, or psy-ops, to prepare studies and speeches that would increase support for the Contra war. A confidential report prepared by psy-ops specialist Colonel Daniel Jacobowitz described the Contras as freedom fighters and outlined themes the president could use to reframe the debate:

> Overall theme: The Nicaraguan Freedom Fighters are fighters for freedom in the American tradition, FSLN are evil. [The Contras are] the good guys . . . the underdogs, [who are deeply] religious. [They also have] anti-Somoza credentials. The Sandinista government, on the other hand, would be cast as an outpost of the Soviet Empire . . . and human rights [violators].

These themes were forwarded to journalists, news networks, editors, educators, and conservative think tanks in government policy papers. In the years that followed, the government message was widely adopted. Newspaper editorials and reports in the media often described Contras as freedom fighters and good guys. The Sandinistas, on the other hand, were almost exclusively described in negative terms by the mainstream press.

Reagan also referred to the Contra forces as freedom fighters in dozens of speeches, and his efforts had the desired effect. While support for the Contras was never widespread, by 1982, about 42 percent of Americans supported the anti-Sandinista efforts.

Building a Force

As Americans began to see the Contras as a positive anti-Soviet force in Central America, the Reagan administration was able to overcome political opposition to funding it. Millions of dollars flowed to the Contras along with tons of weaponry. By late 1982, the FDN had grown to include four to five thousand soldiers. In February and March 1983, they launched large, coordinated offensives in Nicaragua.

Marching past the coffee plantations around Matagalpa, the FDN army moved more than 40 miles (64 km) into the sparsely populated highlands of central Nicaragua. There they established bases and infrastructure to support their army. During the forty-day march, the Contras had split into smaller groups and conducted operations devised by U.S. and Argentinean military planners. The guerrillas attacked state-owned farms, police stations, state-run corporations, ministry posts, and government officials. In the south, Pastora's two thousand ARDE troops conducted similar attacks along the Costa Rica border.

Another front in the Contra war was opened in the swampy lowlands of Nicaragua's Atlantic coast. This region of rivers and jungles is populated by Miskito Indians, indigenous people who belong to the Moravian Protestant Church and speak an English dialect. The Miskitos had fought on the side of the Sandinistas in the revolution. However, afterward, they demanded independence from Nicaragua.

The Sandinistas were opposed to Miskito independence and arrested their leader Steadman Fagoth. The Miskitos demanded Fagoth's release and took over a town on the Atlantic coast in protest. The Sandinistas freed Fagoth, who fled to Honduras with three thousand tribe members. These exiles immediately sought support from the FDN.

By early 1982, the Sandinistas feared an all-out revolution in the mineral- and oil-rich Miskito region. To prevent the area from becoming

A MISKITO INDIAN REFUGEE CHOPS WOOD AT THE REFUGEE CAMP IN HONDURAS IN 1982. MANY OF THE MISKITO PEOPLE FLED NICARAGUA AFTER CLASHES WITH THE SANDINISTA GOVERNMENT.

a Contra stronghold, the Sandinista army conducted its largest military operation to date. The Sandinistas forced about ten thousand people from twenty villages to relocate to urban areas where they would be less likely to organize against the government. The FSLN was said also to have carried out brutal attacks in which eighty-one villages were burned and 250 people were executed. The Sandinistas denied that they had burned the villages and killed the Miskitos.

Nevertheless, Fagoth saw the Sandinistas as the enemy: "I started to look [for] the CIA people. . . . I talked with people in Miami and asked. Someone put me in contact with the CIA. I said: 'I want weapons for the young boys.' That was December 21, 1982." Two months later, the CIA supplied Fagoth with two thousand pairs of boots, $600,000 worth of weapons, and half a million bullets.

Human Rights Controversies

The Sandinistas said the action they took against the Miskitos was necessary to stop counterrevolutionary activities. Critics claimed that the Sandinistas were waging a war on human rights. The Heritage Foundation, a U.S. right-wing organization that had helped develop Reagan's policies in Nicaragua, publicized these accusations. According to a 1983 policy paper by Heritage Foundation analyst Richard Araujo:

> [The] Sandinistas have proved that they surpass their predecessors in abusing the basic rights of their own people in Nicaragua in an all-out war on the human rights of all those who oppose the regime. The victims number in the thousands and include journalists, businessmen, politicians, Catholics, Moravians, the Miskito Indian tribes and even Nicaragua's

> entire Jewish community. . . . There are restrictions on free movement; torture; denial of due process; lack of freedom of thought, conscience and religion; denial of the right of association and of free labor unions.

The allegations made by the Heritage Foundation were often repeated in the press. However, opponents challenged these assertions, claiming they were exaggerated to win broader public support for the war. The organization Human Rights Watch, for example, contradicted the Heritage Foundation after studying the situation in Nicaragua: "Almost invariably, U.S. pronouncements on human rights exaggerated and distorted the real human rights violations of the Sandinista regime, and [ignored] those of the U.S.-supported insurgents, known as the *Contras.*"

Americas Watch, a Catholic group formed to protest training of Latin American military officers in the United States, concluded that the Sandinistas were guilty of abuses against civilians but that there was a "sharp decline" in such incidents after 1982. At the same time, however, documented human rights abuses by the Contras were increasing rapidly. U.S. reporters and human rights groups such as Amnesty International and Witness for Peace accused the paramilitary organization of indiscriminate and brutal attacks on civilians including women, children, and babies.

The Reagan administration denied such claims. However, in October 1984, a piece of evidence came to light that documented abusive Contra tactics. The Associated Press revealed that the Contras had been using a ninety-page training manual called *Psychological Operations in Guerrilla Warfare.* Written by the CIA, this book advocated using "explicit and implicit terror" against the civilian population,

Psychology Operations in Guerrilla Warfare

"OVERALL, THERE IS A conscious effort to reduce the presence of the civilian government, to remove successful social programs and the ideological influence which comes with them. The strategy aims to create the impression of government weakness and *contra* strength. In practice, this means the targeted torture and assassination of teachers, health workers, agricultural technicians and their collaborators in the community. This is not, as many critics charge, 'indiscriminate violence against civilians.' Nor are the killings random acts of terror by incorrigibly brutal ex-National Guardsmen. Rather, the violence is part of a logical and systematic policy, and reflects the changing pattern of the war."
— *Psychological Operations in Guerrilla Warfare*, CIA manual, 1984

including hiring professional criminals to assassinate government employees and civilians. The manual also suggested that the Contras murder their own associates "to create martyrs for the cause."

Contra leader Edgar Chamorro quit the paramilitary organization when he was first given the CIA psy-ops manual. Sickened by the human rights abuses, Chamorro testified before the U.S. House of Representatives, where he described Contra strategies:

> It was premeditated policy to terrorize noncombatants to prevent them from cooperating with the government. Hundreds of civilian murders, mutilations, tortures, and rapes were committed in pursuit of this policy, of which the contra leaders and their CIA superiors were well aware.

Reporters witnessed brutal incidents like those described by Chamorro during a Contra attack on the small town of Ocotal in 1983. Dozens of men, women, and children were killed as soldiers fired machine guns and threw hand grenades into occupied homes.

EDGAR CHAMORRO SPEAKS TO REPORTERS AT HIS HOME IN FLORIDA IN 1985. THE FORMER CONTRA LEADER TESTIFIED BEFORE THE U.S. HOUSE ABOUT HUMAN RIGHTS ABUSES BY THE CONTRAS IN NICARAGUA.

In addition, the Contras destroyed a school, bridges, a lumber mill, and an oil pipeline. After the attack, a farmer spoke to reporter Pete Hamill, saying, "Why are you [Americans] doing this to us?. . . I never learned to read. Now my children are learning to read, and the Yankees send the contras to burn down the school. *Por qué? Por qué?* [Why? Why?]"

> *"The Contras treated civilians as enemies, and on this basis justified their rape, torture, and murder."*
>
> —Robert Kagan, *A Twilight Struggle*, 1996

The CIA War

Operations in small villages caused great damage to Nicaragua. But the Contras lacked the skills to carry out large-scale missions designed to permanently cripple the Sandinista government. These operations were carried out by the U.S. military and the CIA. U.S. forces were aided by mercenary commandos (hired soldiers) called UCLA, or Unilaterally Controlled Latin Assets, recruited from nations throughout the rest of Latin America. One unnamed UCLA described his work: "Our mission was to sabotage ports, refineries, boats and bridges, and try to make it look like the Contras had done it."

This type of sabotage made it clear that the United States was actively working to disrupt life in Nicaragua. The CIA openly operated several ships in the Gulf of Fonseca on Nicaragua's Pacific coast. These were used as bases for Chinook combat helicopters flown by

U.S. pilots and UCLA to strafe and bomb Nicaragua's ports and coastal defenses. In addition, the CIA had total control of Nicaraguan airspace. The CIA used U.S. aircraft equipped with sophisticated radar to provide intelligence to Contras on the ground. This allowed the Contras to avoid the Sandinista army and attack undefended civilian targets, called soft targets.

The Sandinistas tried to fight back by regaining control over their airspace. However, they were unable to get military aircraft from European nations because of the trade embargo. The Soviets were willing to provide aircraft, but the Sandinistas resisted taking them—Ortega did not want to lend support to Reagan's claim that the Soviets were arming the Nicaraguan regime.

Mining the Harbors

One of the most spectacular attacks on Nicaragua was conducted with the aid of U.S. Army Special Forces. Commandos blew up dozens of oil storage tanks containing over 3.2 million gallons (12 millions liters) of gas and diesel fuel, injuring 112 people and forcing 20,000 to evacuate the city of Corinto. Several days later, U.S. Navy Seals blew up a coastal oil pipeline in Puerto Sandino. In the aftermath of the attack, the Exxon Oil Corporation refused to provide tankers to Nicaragua to transport oil. This created major gas shortages and dealt a severe blow to the Nicaraguan economy.

CIA director William Casey was happy with the success of the anti-Sandinista missions. He asked agent Duane "Dewey" Clarridge, who was running the Contra war, to think up new ways to harm Nicaragua's economy. Because the country was dependent on international trade, Clarridge suggested mining the country's harbors. This would damage ships that moved products in and out of Nicaragua. As Clarridge stated, "Cut off shipping and the economy would die."

The idea was to frighten off vessels of countries and companies that traded with Nicaragua, especially those from Mexico that brought in most of the nation's oil. To avoid harming seamen who worked on the ships, the CIA built small "firecracker" mines. Allegedly, these naval mines would not sink ships or kill anyone.

The U.S. mining operation began in January 1984, but the first reports did not appear in the U.S. press until March. This happened after several European and Latin American ships reported damage from the explosive underwater devises. On March 21, a naval mine blew a hole in a Soviet oil tanker approaching Puerto Sandino, injuring five sailors. The Soviets called the mining a "grave crime" and "an act of banditry and piracy," but the United States denied placing the mines. The Contras, however, were eager to take credit even though they lacked the technical expertise and the equipment necessary to lay the mines underwater.

Throughout the spring of 1984, merchant ships from Japan, Panama, Liberia, and the Netherlands were damaged approaching three Nicaraguan ports. A total of fifteen sailors were injured, and two Nicaraguan fishers were killed when their small boat hit a mine and sank.

An Act of War

Laying mines in another nation's harbor is an act of war. Both the United States and the United Nations consider it state-sponsored terrorism. When the mining operation was revealed, even the Contra's strongest congressional supporters were embarrassed. Arizona

Judgment of the International Court of Justice

AFTER THE CIA MINED its harbors, the Nicaraguan government sued the United States in the International Court of Justice in The Hague, Netherlands. Also called the World Court, it was established after World War II as part of the UN charter to moderate disputes between nations.

The case was called *The Republic of Nicaragua v. The United States of America*. Sandinista commander Luis Carrion was called to testify under oath concerning the U.S. role in the mining operation. Carrion said the operation was coordinated from CIA ships in international waters. CIA employees used specially equipped speedboats to lay the mines.

The World Court decided in favor of the Sandinistas in 1986. The court stated that the United States had violated rules of international law by supporting the Contras and mining the harbors. The United States was ordered to stop supporting the counterrevolutionaries and to pay Nicaragua for the damages caused by the mines. Reagan refused to accept the judgment. The American ambassador to the UN, Jeane Kirkpatrick, spoke for the administration when she dismissed the court ruling: "The [International Court of Justice], quite frankly, is not what its name suggests, an international court of justice. It's a semi-legal, semi-juridical, semi-political body which nations sometimes accept and sometimes don't."

Republican senator Barry Goldwater, who had been a loyal champion of the Reagan Doctrine, said, "I feel like a fool. . . . I feel betrayed." Casey apologized to Goldwater, and the mining operation was halted.

The mining of the harbors created a major backlash against the war in the U.S. Congress. To stop Contra funding, Massachusetts

> *"The United States policies constitute the most serious violation of the rules of international law that forbid intervention in the internal affairs of others."*
>
> —judgment of the International Court of Justice in *The Republic of Nicaragua v. The United States of America*, 1985

Democrat Edward Patrick Boland had introduced an amendment to a military funding bill that specifically outlawed U.S. assistance to the CIA for the purpose of overthrowing the government of Nicaragua. However, Reagan condemned the Boland Amendment, saying, "Those people who shut off that aid are supporting a totalitarian dictatorship in Nicaragua."

The administration ignored the Boland Amendment and used other military funds to supply the Contras. In this manner, they provided the paramilitary force with $54 million in 1983. However, in 1984, another version of the Boland Amendment was passed by the House of Representatives that explicitly outlawed any support for the Contras through any branch of the government. Reagan had little choice but to sign the bill, which had passed by an overwhelming vote of 411–0.

Elections in Two Nations

When the Boland Amendment passed, Reagan was in the middle of a contentious election campaign, and the war was becoming increasingly unpopular. Coincidentally, there was also an election campaign in Nicaragua. The Sandinistas had finally honored their pledge to hold democratic elections. In late 1983, Ortega had announced that voting would take place on November 4, 1984, two days before the election in the United States. To prepare for the event, the Sandinistas sent commissions to the United States and Western Europe to study electoral procedures and laws. However, the date Ortega picked for Nicaraguan elections was controversial in the United States. Government officials in the United States complained that opposition parties would not have enough time to organize against Ortega, who was running for president. Reagan denounced the elections as a "Soviet-style farce."

People line up to vote in the 1984 presidential election in Nicaragua. The election process was observed by experts from different parts of the world.

Democrats in Congress who opposed the war supported the Nicaragua election. They wanted to see the nation lawfully elect a president for the first time in the nation's history. Democrat Jim Wright of Texas sent Ortega a letter, signed by several other members of Congress, that said, "We write with hope that you . . . guarantee a fully open and democratic electoral process. . . . [If so, those] responsible for supporting violence against your government [in the Reagan administration] would have a far greater difficulty winning support for their policies than they do today."

Within the Reagan administration, there was fear that the election of a popular leader like Ortega would give the Sandinistas international legitimacy. The Sandinistas were quite popular at home for their health, labor, and education programs. Therefore, the CIA was given the task of making the elections seem illegitimate. Walker describes the process:

> U.S. officials in Nicaragua were working feverishly behind the scenes to cajole, counsel, pressure, and, reportedly, bribe the candidates of the six opposition parties that were formally registered in election to withdraw.

The election was closely watched by impartial experts sent by the British and Irish parliaments, the Dutch government, and the Latin American Studies Association, located in the United States. All observers agreed that the election was fair and the votes were legitimately counted. Ortega was elected the legitimate president of Nicaragua in the eyes of the international community. However, because the main opposition parties did not participate, the victory was not viewed as legitimate by leaders in the United States who refused to accept the outcome.

CHAPTER 6

The End of the Sandinistas

IN MAY 1985, BOTH HOUSES of Congress passed Boland II. This law banned funding for any military activity against Nicaragua for a period of two years. President Reagan was determined to continue the Contra war, however. He asked his national security adviser, Robert McFarlane, to think of ways to fund the Contras until Congress could be convinced to strike down Boland II.

McFarlane appointed Marine lieutenant colonel Oliver North to the National Security Council (NSC) staff and asked him to carry out the president's wishes. North began a top-secret program to fund the Contras, using donations from wealthy individuals and foreign governments. With these efforts, North raised $32 million from Saudi Arabian leaders and $10 million from the sultan of Brunei, the richest man in the world at that time. To manage the money, North set up a series of fake companies and used them to open secret Swiss bank accounts. The money was then diverted from Switzerland to the Contras in Nicaragua.

Even as the United States escalated the war in Nicaragua, Latin American leaders were working for peace. Diplomats from Mexico, Venezuela, Colombia, and Panama met on Contadora Island in Panama to draw up an agreement to end the Contra war. They hoped to negotiate a peace settlement between the Sandinistas and the Contras. The United States would then be forced to agree with the results.

When the Contadora process first began in 1983, Reagan refused to become involved. He believed that the Sandinistas could not be trusted to follow any accord. However, by the mid-1980s, the Reagan administration was using the Contadora negotiations as leverage to bargain for more funding for the Contras. As Elliott Abrams, assistant secretary of state for inter-American affairs, told the *New York Times*: "If you want the Contadora process to . . . succeed, we believe that the only way to do it is through the military pressure that the contras can put on the Sandinista regime. . . . If there's no pressure, they're not going to negotiate, they're not going to compromise."

"A Neat Idea"

North could not wait for Congress to repeal Boland II. He felt that the Contras were in desperate need of funds. To procure those funds, North arranged to sell HAWK antiaircraft missiles to Iran in November 1985. The sale netted about $30 million for North, of which $18 million was diverted to the Contras in Nicaragua. The rest of the money, according to a government report, remained unaccounted for.

The missile sale to Iran was in violation of the Arms Export Control Act, which forbade the sale of weapons to terrorist states, such as Iran. In addition, the deal violated Reagan's oft-stated pledge that the United States would never deal with terrorists. North later said, "I thought using the [Ayatollah Khomeini's] money to support the Nicaraguan resistance was a neat idea." However, the operation, known as the Iran-Contra Affair, would become one of the major scandals of the Reagan presidency.

Reagan later claimed he was unaware of North's plan. However, he was also working to raise money for the Contras from outside sources. In early 1985, the president attended a series of fund-raisers hosted by the nation's largest conservative political organizations. At these events, some of the United States' wealthiest citizens donated millions of dollars to the Contra cause. Contributors included Joseph Coors, CEO of Coors Brewing Company; Reverend Sun Myung Moon, leader of the Unification Church and owner of the *Washington Times*; and Lew Lehrman, Rite Aid drugstore heir.

On March 1, 1985, Reagan attended a fund-raiser hosted by the Conservative Political Action Committee where he compared the Contras to George Washington and Thomas Jefferson: "They are our brothers, these freedom fighters, and we owe them our help. . . . They are the moral equal of our Founding Fathers and the brave men and women of the French Resistance [who fought the Nazis in World War II]. We cannot turn away from them, for the struggle here is not right versus left; it is right versus wrong."

In addition to fund-raising, Reagan continued to apply political pressure on congressional representatives. The president stated that he might order the U.S. Marines to invade Nicaragua if Congress refused to fund the Contras. Backing his words with action, the president ordered a series of joint military maneuvers in Central America.

The Iran-Contra Affair

ON NOVEMBER 3, 1986, a Lebanese magazine reported that the United States had sold arms to Iran in 1985. At first President Reagan denied the arms deal had taken place. However, political pressure soon forced the president to confirm the story in a televised speech on November 13, 1986. Reagan found himself in the worst public relations disaster of his presidency. At a November 19 press conference, he appeared unsteady and confused and made several factual errors concerning the Iran affair. Two days later, Attorney General Edwin Meese agreed to initiate a formal inquiry into the matter. When North heard news of the inquest, he told McFarlane that he was going to have a shredding party to destroy documents that mentioned the affair. Meese soon confirmed that the money from the arms sale had been used for military aid to the Contras in 1985 and 1986 in violation of the Boland Amendment.

As a result of the Iran-Contra affair, Reagan's public approval rating dropped from 67 to 46 percent nearly overnight, and opponents called for his impeachment. Reagan was not impeached, but North was indicted on multiple charges concerning the Iran-Contra affair. However, after many court battles, the case was dismissed on legal technicalities.

Oliver North testifies before Congress in 1987 about the Iran-Contra affair.

These exercises took place in Honduras with tens of thousands of U.S. and Latin American troops. Maneuvers included amphibious (water-based) landings, mock bombings, and live-fire exercises meant to intimidate the Sandinistas.

The U.S. media also talked of an invasion. In June 1985, the *New York Times* ran an item called "An Invasion Is Openly Discussed." The article quoted intelligence sources that said the United States could easily rout the Sandinistas. Colonel William Comee Jr., director of operations for the U.S. Southern Command, explained, "Major Nicaraguan installations are lightly defended. . . . With minimal risk, American pilots could destroy the small Nicaraguan Air Force, radar, artillery, tanks, supply depots and command centers. . . . [It] would take the United States two weeks to gain control of 60 percent of the Nicaraguan population. . . . The Sandinistas would be up in the hills, but that would be a problem for the new Nicaraguan government. It wouldn't be our problem."

The Price of Invasion

AFTER COLONEL WILLIAM COMEE Jr. claimed that a small U.S. military force could conquer Nicaragua in two weeks with minimal casualties, a Pentagon (headquarters of the U.S. Department of Defense) study contradicted Comee's statement, saying it would take a force of 125,000 troops to oust the Sandinistas. This would result in 3,000 to 4,000 U.S. casualties in the first few days. An additional 10,000 to 20,000 soldiers would be wounded, and the cost would be more than $10 billion. These numbers were unacceptable to military planners, who did not feel Americans would support such an expensive and bloody operation.

On the Sandinista Home Front

The aggressive actions of the United States made the Sandinista leadership extremely nervous. But even without a U.S. invasion, the Contra war was having an extremely negative effect on the Nicaraguan people. By 1985 the United States had declared a total trade embargo against Nicaragua. This prevented Nicaraguan products such as sugar, bananas, and coffee from reaching markets in the United States and elsewhere. The embargo, combined with the damages from the war, nearly bankrupted the Nicaraguan government. In 1985 the Sandinistas put their direct economic losses at about $660 million figured in 2007 dollars, with indirect losses at $2.6 billion. This sum was equal to the nation's entire export earnings during the previous four years.

The damage to the Nicaraguan economy came at a time when the Sandinistas were using 50 percent of the entire national budget for defense. This money was spent on military hardware such as helicopters, artillery, antiaircraft equipment, troop transports, and light weaponry purchased from the various Communist countries.

The war had social costs as well. By now many Nicaraguans felt that the government should try to negotiate a settlement to end the war. When the Sandinistas instituted a draft instead, the move was extremely unpopular. The draft did, however, help increase the size of the Nicaraguan army from about forty thousand troops to eighty thousand troops. The government also expanded the Sandinista militia, a sixty-thousand-member civilian organization that was equipped with AK-47 automatic rifles to fight the Contras. These forces were able to prevent the Contras from seizing and holding a single town where they might establish a new government. However, the counterrevolutionaries were able to continue their operations with little opposition in northcentral Nicaragua.

Continuing with Reform

Even with a war going on, the Sandinistas continued to implement their social programs, directing scarce funds to agriculture and health care. Most agricultural reform concerned the resettlement of peasants from isolated war-torn regions to cooperative farms in safer areas. According to a former Peace Corps worker in Nicaragua, Harvey Williams, this "was viewed as mostly positive. [The peasants] ended up with more and better land and were less vulnerable to the attacks of the counterrevolutionaries, and they received the benefits of the government programs in health, education, welfare, and housing." Some, however, believed that the forced relocations were really undertaken to keep antigovernment peasants from joining the Contras.

> *"While the [Nicaraguan] government claimed it was moving the peasants to protect them from being raped and kidnapped by the Contras, in fact the program was intended to get the peasants where they could be controlled more easily."*
>
> —Contra fighter Roger Miranda and policy analyst William Ratliff in *The Civil War in Nicaragua*, 1993

Whatever the case, the Sandinistas also continued to emphasize health care, even during the worst years of the war between 1983 and 1986. The Ministry of Health continued its rural programs, using donations from international relief organizations such as CARE, Oxfam America, American Friends Service Committee, and Church World Service. These programs emphasized preventive health care, early

NICARAGUAN CHILDREN POSE IN A RELOCATION CENTER IN THE LATE 1980S. MANY PEASANTS WERE MOVED TO NEW LOCATIONS BY THE SANDINISTA GOVERNMENT.

treatment of disease, mass immunizations, and reduction of infant mortality. About five hundred Cuban doctors and an equal number of physicians from North America and Europe aided MINSA. The Contras kidnapped twenty-eight of these volunteer health professionals and wounded an additional eleven. The Contras also destroyed or forced the closure of about one hundred health clinics.

The shipping embargo prevented doctors from obtaining important medications and parts for broken medical equipment. Without these supplies, health workers found it difficult to treat the five thousand people who had been wounded by the Contras.

TARGETING HEALTH WORKERS

The Contras killed about eleven thousand Nicaraguans before 1985, including thirty-five health-care providers. Two male doctors, from France and West Germany, were murdered in September 1985, after the Contras raped and shot the female nurses who worked with them. Such actions were in clear violation of the Geneva Conventions that govern international rules of war. However, a Contra radio station announced in August 1985 that "all foreigners who come to implant communism in Nicaragua [are regarded] as legitimate targets."

Five thousand local health-care workers were either drafted or mobilized to aid in the national defense. This meant fewer doctors, nurses, and volunteers were available for the civilian population. As a result, there was a dramatic increase in treatable diseases such as measles and malaria. Mosquito-borne dengue fever showed a major resurgence. Many thought Sandinista programs had eliminated dengue fever in 1982. But in 1985, an epidemic swept through the country, sickening about half the population of Managua.

"Hard Won Social Progress"

Unlike health services, the Sandinistas sharply curtailed educational programs between 1983 and 1986. During this period, about ninety-three thousand students, or 10 percent of the nation's total, had to stop attending school. These students either were drafted, were forced to go to work, or found their school buildings destroyed by the Contras. Even so, teachers were given small raises, and the number of scholarships provided for poor students increased.

Much of the funding for education was diverted to other programs related to the war. For example, the conflict orphaned more than seven thousand children by 1985. While family or friends cared for most, about twelve hundred were provided with pensions by the government. The Sandinistas also opened about 180 child care centers and children's nutrition centers to eliminate hunger among the poor.

Commenting on the success of many social programs the Sandinistas undertook during the war, Peace Corps worker Williams concludes:

> It was notable that a government with such limited resources could make as much progress in so many areas within the first seven years after coming to power. It was remarkable that Nicaragua achieved these accomplishments while defending against the aggression of one of the most powerful nations on earth. . . . Although serious problems and limitations remained, even beyond the aggression of the counterrevolutionaries and the Reagan administration, it was unlikely that any power would easily be able to take away the hard won social progress of the Nicaraguan people.

Funding the Contras

The hard-won reforms would be seriously tested. The Contra war was in its third year, and the Nicaraguan economy was struggling. The United States had convinced Mexico and Venezuela to stop selling oil to Nicaragua. This meant the Sandinistas had to obtain their oil from the Soviet Union in trade for Nicaraguan sugar, coffee, and bananas.

Forced to turn to the Soviet Union for aid, Ortega journeyed to Moscow, Russia, and five other Communist countries in March 1985. Although this was not Ortega's first trip to Moscow, the trip was roundly criticized in the United States, where it was used as an excuse to resume Contra funding. Reagan stated that Ortega's trip was a "national emergency [because of Nicaragua's] unusual and extraordinary threat to the national security and foreign policy of the United States."

Ortega's Moscow trip was the main topic of debate when the

NICARAGUAN PRESIDENT DANIEL ORTEGA *(IN LIGHT COAT)* VISITED MOSCOW IN 1985 TO SECURE AID FOR HIS COUNTRY. THE TRIP WAS HOTLY DEBATED IN THE U.S. CONGRESS.

House of Representatives passed a bill granting $27 million in humanitarian aid to the Contras. (Humanitarian aid is supposed to be used for medicine and food, road building and construction, but not for military purposes.) A few weeks later, the Senate added more money to the House aid package bringing the total to $38 million. Commenting on the tone of the debate, Republican senator Mark Hatfield from Oregon commented, "We had a hate-in—everybody said 'I hate the Sandinistas more than you do; I just hate them differently.'"

The following year, the Reagan administration asked for an unprecedented $100 million in military aid to the Contras. The House voted against the proposal. However, in early 1986, the Sandinista army crossed into Honduras to strike Contra camps along the border. This was seen in the United States as an act of war against Honduras. Following this event, Congress approved the $100 million in June with $70 million intended specifically for weapons.

The Hasenfus Affair

Despite the influx of money, the Contras faced major problems that limited their military impact on the Sandinistas. For example, they had only six run-down transport planes from the Somoza era. This made it difficult for them to airdrop supplies to Contra fighters inside Nicaragua. To improve the situation, the CIA secretly rented airplanes and hired Americans to aid with the airdrops. However, this proved to be a strategic blunder when one of the Contra supply planes was shot down on October 5, 1986. The two Latin American pilots died in the crash, but one of the crew members parachuted to the ground and turned himself in to the Sandinistas. His name was Eugene Hasenfus, and he was an American working for the Contras. Hasenfus was the first American captured in the war. His presence proved beyond a doubt that the United States was involved in military missions within Nicaragua.

Eugene Hasenfus, an American who worked for the Contras, went on trial in 1986 for war crimes in Nicaragua. He was convicted and sentenced to thirty years in prison but was later released by Daniel Ortega.

> *"Since [the Sandinistas] captured me, every day these people could be doing whatever they want to me, I believe with justification. And they have treated me well."*
>
> —Eugene Hasenfus, private contractor for the CIA, in an interview with *60 Minutes*, 1976

The Sandinistas arrested Hasenfus. He was charged with committing war crimes, given a quick trial, and sentenced to thirty years in prison. However, just before Christmas 1986, Daniel Ortega released the American to a visiting U.S. senator, Christopher Dodd of Connecticut, a war opponent. Ortega called the release of Hasenfus an act of "charity and good will," but his brother Humberto admitted it was a propaganda victory for the Sandinistas: "We got a lot more good out of this war criminal by turning him over to Dodd than we would have by letting him rot for years in jail."

The timing of the Hasenfus affair could not have been worse for the Reagan administration. Less than a month after Hasenfus's capture, the news finally broke that members of the Reagan administration had illegally sold weapons to Iran to raise money for the Contras. This occurred at a time when the Boland II Amendment prohibited such activities.

Renewed Fighting

Even as the Iran-Contra scandal unfolded, the Sandinistas were forging ahead with efforts to remake Nicaragua. In January 1987, the National Assembly adopted a democratic constitution. This document, which is still in effect in 2009, created an executive branch with a president elected by popular vote to a six-year term—shortened to five years in 1995. Legislative power is vested in a ninety-three-member National Constituent Assembly elected to six-year terms. There are no restrictions on political parties. Since the constitution was enacted, vast numbers of candidates from a wide political spectrum have run for the offices of president, positions in the National Assembly, and local municipality posts.

The Sandinista People's Army also continued to repel efforts by the Contras. FSLN commanders plotted a winning strategy based on an unlikely source—U.S. Army counterinsurgency manuals. These manuals instructed commanders to create Irregular Warfare Battalions (BLIs) and Light Hunter Battalions (BCLs). Sandinistas in these elite fighting forces used army tactics to attack Contras in their strongholds along the Honduras border.

The renewed military efforts were expensive, and the total cost of the war was bankrupting Nicaragua. Between 1981 and 1987, the United States spent a sum equal to about half a billion dollars to fund the Contras. To defend themselves, the Sandinistas spent $9 billion. This great expense caused the Nicaraguan unit of currency, the córdoba, to crash. Because the money was nearly worthless, prices rose to astronomical levels. By 1988 the inflation rate was 33,000 percent. An item that cost 1 cordoba in 1980 cost 330 cordobas eight years later.

Most Nicaraguans were unable to afford the most basic necessities of life. To bring down the inflation rate, the Sandinistas were forced to cut almost all government spending beyond defense. As a result, thousands of government workers found themselves unemployed and bitter.

Impact on the Grassroots Movement

During this time of financial crises, participation in grassroots groups—the centerpiece of the Sandinista movement—plummeted. The citizen groups were originally formed to promote the wishes of the majority and address complaints against the government. However, by this time, duties of the OPs had been transformed. The Sandinistas used the OPs as a tool to resist the Contras and preserve political power. For example, neighborhood committees that once planned garbage pickups and Saturday night dances were put in charge of recruiting young men for the unpopular military draft. Union groups, rather than addressing the needs of labor, were asked by the government to urge workers to take pay cuts and work longer hours to defend the country. This created widespread unhappiness with the organizations, and group membership fell drastically.

Making Peace

In August 1987, Costa Rican president Oscar Arias offered a peace plan to provide relief to the Nicaraguan people. It was negotiated after six months of heated debate between representatives of Guatemala, El Salvador, Honduras, Nicaragua, and the United States. The Arias Peace Plan called for an immediate cease-fire and for free elections to be held in 1990 with international supervision. The Sandinistas and the Contras agreed to the Arias plan, and it was signed on March 23, 1988. That same year, Arias was awarded the Nobel Peace Prize for his efforts.

Political prisoners in Nicaragua line up to receive certificate of liberty papers from government officials in November 1987. The Sandinistas released the prisoners in accordance with the Arias Peace Plan.

With the signing of the Arias plan, the war was over, but Nicaraguans had paid a heavy price. The conflict resulted in the deaths of more than 30,900 people—21,900 Contras, 4,860 government troops, and 4,150 civilians. Walker explains the significance behind the statistics: "Calculating roughly that the population of Nicaragua . . . averaged about 3.3 million during the war years, the over 30,000 dead represented 0.9 percent of the population. An equivalent loss for the United States would be 2.25 million or over thirty-eight times the U.S. death toll in the entire Vietnam War. The war also produced 20,064 wounded, many of them so permanently disabled that they would be wards of the state for the rest of their lives."

The Arias Peace Plan

THE ARIAS PEACE PLAN called for dialogue between governments and opposition groups, amnesty for political prisoners, cease-fires in ongoing insurgent conflicts, and free elections in all five regional states. In addition, opposition parties would be guaranteed freedom of the press and access to radio and television. The plan also called for renewed negotiations on arms reductions and a ban on outside aid to insurgent forces.

On March 12, 1987, the U.S. Senate endorsed the Arias Peace Plan with a nearly unanimous vote of 97–1. Reagan lambasted the plan as too lenient on the Sandinistas, but the momentum toward peace could not be stopped. On August 6, presidents from all five Central American nations gathered at the Guatemalan National Palace in Esquipulas. Arias read the text, and the presidents signed what was by then called the Procedure for a Firm and Lasting Peace in Central America.

In Nicaragua the Sandinistas implemented cease-fire negotiations with the Contras. The talks quickly bogged down, and there was sporadic fighting on both sides. In the meantime, the Sandinistas lifted the state of emergency and released prisoners of war. Negotiations dragged for months. Finally, the Contras agreed to disarm on January 31, 1989, eleven days after Ronald Reagan's presidential term ended.

Why the Contras Lost

The Contras caused great misery in Nicaragua, seriously damaging the nation's economy and the political fortunes of the Sandinistas. However, the paramilitary force failed on several levels in their quest to reclaim the country.

Politically, the Contras never presented the Nicaraguan people with a positive alternative to the Sandinistas. Rather than offering appealing educational or agricultural programs to attract support, the counterrevolutionaries waged a war of violence and attrition (harassment and abuse). This led people to believe the Contras were nothing but a loose affiliation of former Somoza supporters carrying out the wishes of the U.S. imperialists. The image was further reinforced when the CIA appointed former National Guard leader Enrique Bermúdez as military chief of the FDN.

The Contras and their CIA backers also made tactical errors. For example, the counterrevolutionaries chose to avoid cities and fight in the countryside. Therefore, the FDN never engaged the Sandinistas in the cities where their power was based. The CIA could be blamed for the public relations disaster that resulted from mining Nicaragua's harbors. This audacious and illegal mission produced little in the way of military success, but it galvanized the opponents of the Contra war in the United States and in the rest of the world.

Despite the loss, the Contras took a heavy toll on the Sandinista social experiment. As the Reagan administration neared its end in 1988, Daniel Ortega's grasp on power was slipping away. After more than ten years of war, many Nicaraguans were ready for change.

CHAPTER 7

The Chamorro Years

THROUGHOUT THE 1980S, political dialogue in the United States was often dominated by tough talk against Cuban and Soviet Communists and Nicaraguan Marxists. However, as the 1980s drew to a close, a series of unexpected events changed the entire world. In the autumn of 1989, Soviet domination of Eastern Europe collapsed within the space of a few months. People in Hungary, Poland, East Germany, Romania, Czechoslovakia, and Bulgaria were free to choose their own leaders after suffering under totalitarian Communist regimes for about fifty years.

The collapse of European Communism also had a major impact on Nicaragua. Daniel Ortega had traveled widely in Eastern Europe. He was close to many of the now-deposed leaders and had worked out economic pacts with their governments. The Soviet Union itself was teetering on the brink of bankruptcy and would dissolve in 1991, ending the long Cold War standoff with the United States. In the meantime, Soviet leader Mikhail Gorbachev declared his nation was no longer interested in supporting a worldwide Communist revolution. The Soviets had been giving about $800 million in aid to the Sandinistas annually and had provided Nicaragua with nearly all of its oil. This support ended.

Election 90

Even as Daniel Ortega struggled with this new reality, he was engaged in a bitter battle with the Contras over the Arias Peace Accord. Although Reagan was out of office, the new U.S. president, George H. W. Bush, continued to push for support of the Contras. Bush also wanted to keep pressure on Ortega until Nicaragua's next presidential election, which was scheduled for January 1991. Congress agreed with the Bush strategy and approved $55 million in aid for the Contras in 1989. However, Democrats attached conditions to the funding. The Contras would have to support the peace process, refrain from launching attacks, and continue to demobilize, that is, discharge military personnel and send them home. Meanwhile, Republicans pushed for laws to ensure that the trade embargo against Nicaragua remained in place. They also maintained their forceful anti-Sandinista rhetoric in speeches.

The events in the United States, Eastern Europe, and the Soviet Union had a direct effect on Ortega's second run for president. Nicaragua was bitterly divided, and Ortega needed to heal the nation's wounds quickly. To do so, he loosened wartime restrictions on opposition parties and implemented civil rights guaranteed in the 1987 constitution. The president ended wartime censorship so anti-Sandinista newspapers and magazines could publish without restrictions.

As the opposition to the Sandinistas grew stronger, there were demands that Ortega call for an early election. Much to everyone's surprise, he agreed. The president set an election date for February 25, 1990, and reversed measures put in place in 1984 that were meant to ensure a Sandinista victory. For example, the Sandinistas would allow anyone to run for office, even former Contras. All parties would receive state financing and would be given free time weekly on Nicaragua's two television channels. For one hour each night, a program called *Election 90* featured debates between two parties chosen by lots.

The National Opposition Union

Ortega's opponents did not want to see a rerun of the 1984 election, where two dozen opposition parties splintered the anti-Sandinista vote. To avoid this in 1990, the United States sent advisers to Nicaragua to unite the opposition into a single party, the National Opposition Union, or UNO. The party included members from fourteen of the twenty-two widely diverse anti-Sandinista parties from across the political spectrum. For example, UNO united the pro-U.S. National Action Party, the conservative Social Democratic Party, and the Communist Party of Nicaragua under one banner. After a bitter fight over who to nominate as the head of the party, UNO members picked Violeta Chamorro.

Chamorro was not the ideal candidate. She was not articulate, was often unaware of important issues, and seemed unconcerned about political strategies. Nevertheless, Chamorro proved to be a wise choice for UNO. She was not a Sandinista, she was well-known as the editor of a popular anti-Sandinista newspapers, her husband had been assassinated by the Samozas, and she was not caught up in political battles.

"Nicaragua is so desperate and I am certain of giving you the hope which does not depend on me alone, but on all of us together, working as a single team, a single force, invincible in the face of disloyalty and enemy attacks, because when one does good, evil flees defeated by the face of God."

—Violeta Chamorro, 1990

Chamorro had the strong backing of the United States. And although the Sandinistas had ample money to fund Ortega's reelection, it appeared that he could be defeated. Therefore, the United States spent millions of dollars to support Chamorro and other UNO candidates. The CIA launched a $6 million covert program to train UNO activists in Costa Rica and gave $600,000 to former Contras to run election campaigns. The agency also funded a media operation to vilify the Sandinistas, broadcasting propaganda from radio stations based in Costa Rica.

The United States spent another $11 million to fund opposition parties and to boost voter registration. In all, the Bush administration spent about $7 per Nicaraguan voter, the modern equivalent of $800 million. Bush made numerous statements endorsing Chamorro. He promised to end support for the Contras and call off the embargo if the UNO candidate won.

A Referendum on Sandinista Rule

UNO was handicapped by internal bickering and limited popularity.

However, a vote for Chamorro meant an end to the war and the U.S. embargo. The choice was clear for voters.

Most Nicaraguans earned less than twenty dollars a month and were deprived of the basic necessities. Rice, beans, coffee, toilet paper, soap, and toothpaste were often unavailable for two or three months at a time. Ortega tried to remedy this situation before the election, asking the Soviet Union for aid. According to Yuri Pavlov, an official in the Soviet Foreign Ministry, the Sandinistas "wanted money to put consumer goods in the stores, so they could portray the economic situation as improving and attract voter support. . . . We didn't think it was a good investment." Despite Pavlov's statement, almost everyone, including the Bush administration, the press corps, and even opposition candidates, expected the Sandinistas to retain power.

A woman takes one of the last bags of rice from an empty supermarket shelf in June 1989. Basic necessities were often scarce in the late 1980s in Nicaragua.

As the 1990 election approached, more than two thousand election observers from the United Nations and the Organization of American States poured into Nicaragua. Former president Jimmy Carter joined those who were there to monitor the vote.

For their part, Nicaraguan voters had to decide whether or not they were happy with ten years of Sandinista rule. Many blamed the country's horrible economy on the FSLN. To counter this belief, the Sandinistas linked the economic problems to the war. They also im-

UNO presidential candidate Violeta Chamorro campaigns in February 1990. Chamorro's candidacy was supported by the United States.

"By focusing on the war, the Sandinistas hoped to escape, Houdini-like, from the political consequences of the country's [economic] collapse. It didn't work."

—William Leogrande, political adviser, commenting on the 1990 Nicaragua presidential election, 1998

plied that the UNO was closely backed by the Contras and the U.S. imperialists. Observers expected an extremely close contest, and the stakes could not have been higher for the Sandinistas.

On February 25, an amazing 86 percent of Nicaragua's voters cast ballots. Chamorro won by a large margin, defying expectations. She attracted 55 percent of the vote compared with Ortega's 41 percent, and UNO also captured a majority of seats in the National Assembly.

On April 25, 1990, Violeta Chamorro was inaugurated president at the National Stadium in Managua. Even at this solemn moment, it was obvious that Nicaraguans remained angry and divided. During the ceremony, UNO supporters sat on one side of the stadium and Sandinistas on the other. The two groups booed and hissed at each other throughout the ceremonies. However, the Sandinistas made history by respecting the election results. It was the first peaceful transfer of power in Nicaragua in almost sixty years.

Some analysts considered the democratic change of power to be a Sandinista success. According to the Central American Historical Institute at Georgetown University in Washington, D.C.: "[The] big victor, the big winner of these elections is the Sandinista Front, which brought democracy to Nicaragua. Without the Sandinista Front the Nicaraguan people would never have dreamed of elections such

"Many observers have argued that the Nicaraguan revolution failed, since the Sandinista Front was voted out of power. I, on the other hand, would maintain the opposite. . . . Without doubt, the credit for institutionalizing electoral democracy in Nicaragua belongs to the Sandinistas. From a traditional Western perspective, which focuses on political democracy, the Sandinista experiment has to be considered successful."

—Ilja A. Luciak, *The Sandinista Legacy*, 1995

as those which occurred on February 25, 1990." The Sandinistas though, who were totally surprised by their loss, didn't see it as a victory.

Whatever the case, people remained anxious after the inauguration. Many expected former Somoza and Contra supporters to overthrow the new president and take Nicaragua back to a dictatorship. Victoria, a thirty-six-year-old Nicaraguan housewife, described the situation:

> It was quite tense, especially those first several weeks. There were no guarantees that the contras would lay down their arms. What if they changed their minds? It was as if the whole country held its breath, and every day that went by, we let out a little sigh of relief.

Holding the Country Together

Chamorro tried to ensure government stability in several ways. After her election, she worked closely with the Sandinistas. Together, the opposing parties established ground rules to guarantee a smooth change of power between the old government and the new. Chamorro also went to great efforts to make sure disarmament and demobilization accords were carried out between the Sandinista People's Army and FDN.

Chamorro refused demands from the Bush administration to put in place a plan called deSandinistaization. This program would rid the government of all former officials. Instead, Chamorro made a deal with former minister of defense Humberto Ortega. He could retain his position if he demobilized most of the military. Ortega agreed, and within a year, the army was reduced from eighty thousand to seventeen thousand troops.

With a stable peace at hand, money began to flow into Nicaragua. There was an influx of foreign aid from the United States and other democracies. Large corporations, which had been thrown out by the Sandinistas, began investing in Nicaragua once again. With new money from taxes and aid, Chamorro was able to stabilize the gold córdoba, which replaced the Sandinista córdoba. This lowered inflation considerably.

Chamorro's economic program for Nicaragua included measures that reduced government expenses. Her administration made drastic cuts in the health, education, and agricultural programs established by the Sandinistas. Thousands of government workers lost their jobs.

Despite the economic pain her programs inflicted on many

workers, Chamorro was viewed as a moderate. Having worked with both the Sandinistas in the early days of the revolution and the opposition in later years, the new president was able to forge bonds between the left and right.

> *"Nicaragua experienced unprecedented freedom of expression and the gradual, [if] fragile, pacification of the country."*
>
> —Cynthia Chavez Metoyer, specialist on women in Latin American politics, commenting on Violeta Chamorro's presidential term, 2000

The Recontras and the Recompas

Chamorro was given credit for acting in a nonpartisan manner with the military. She worked with Humberto Ortega to demobilize the Sandinista's People's Army and changed its name to the National Army. This helped defuse the revolutionary nature of the military. However, when the tens of thousands of soldiers were released, it created other serious problems. The soldiers, many of them young men, had little experience outside the military and were left unemployed and homeless.

Former Contras, in particular, were unprepared for civilian life. About 83 percent of the FDN consisted of poor peasants and laborers from the north and central regions of the country. Only 25 percent had been property owners, 60 percent were under twenty-five, and 90 percent were semiliterate or illiterate. The Arias Peace Accord promised these men land and resettlement benefits. However, Nicaragua remained poor, and the foreign aid promised by the Bush administration, according to historian Walker, "was trivial given the economic damage the United States had inflicted on Nicaragua." As a result, the former soldiers banded together to pressure Chamorro to honor the promises of the peace plan.

The demobilized Contras were known as *recontras*, demobilized Sandinistas were called *recompas*, and mixed groups from both sides were called *revueltos*. Many of these ex-soldiers supported themselves through banditry, kidnapping, drug running, and paid assassination. They terrorized the countryside, taking control of small towns, public buildings, roadways, and private lands. By mid-1992, there were about twenty-two thousand rearmed soldiers from both sides operating in Nicaragua. Many of them were based in the former Contra strongholds in the northern part of the country.

Most of the violence perpetrated by the recontras and recompas was random. However, some of it was politically inspired. For example, on July 21, 1993, about 150 recompas, calling themselves the Revolutionary Front of Workers and Peasants (FROC) took over the town of Estelí. They demanded that Chamorro grant them property titles, access to education, health care, and jobs. Rather than negotiate, Chamorro sent in the National Army, which killed 45 FROC members and wounded another 98.

Not long after the Estelí occupation, a double hostage crisis made headlines. In August 1993, a group of recontras called the Northern Front invaded a meeting of government delegates. These officials were FSLN deputies, UNO officials, and members of the Special Disarmament Brigade working to implement aspects of the peace accord. The guerrillas took them all hostage and demanded the dismissal of Humberto Ortega and other Sandinistas still involved in the Chamorro government.

A wounded National Army soldier heads toward an area in the city of Estelí that was occupied by former Sandinista soldiers in July 1993.

In response to the Northern Front action, a group of recompas called the Dignity and Sovereignty Commandos took over UNO headquarters in Managua. After taking several members of a political council hostage, including Vice President Virgilio Godoy, the commandos demanded the release of those detained by the Northern Front. The situation was finally defused when members of UNO and the FSLN acted together to call off the opposing groups.

Neoliberal Economics

It soon became obvious to the ex-soldiers that the Chamorro government had no money to help them. Her administration was deliberately shrinking the government and had few plans to aid the nation's poor. Like many other Latin American countries at the time, Nicaragua was implementing what is called the neoliberal model of economics. The neoliberal model stresses economic growth, minimal government intrusion in the economy, few restrictions on trade, and a free market in which prices of goods and services are set by sellers and buyers rather than the government. This economic model of government was the opposite of the state-regulated Marxist economy promoted by the Sandinistas.

To implement this economic plan, Chamorro spent the first five years of her six-year term downsizing the government. She eliminated tariffs and taxes that restricted foreign companies from operating in Nicaragua. All Sandinista rules regulating private property were repealed. Her administration sold over three hundred state-owned businesses including the national airlines, energy and telecommunications companies, urban businesses, and state farms. Chamorro also passed a law that allowed peasant cooperatives to sell their land, something that had been illegal under the Sandinistas. Because many farmers badly needed money, a large number of cooperatives were sold to giant agribusiness companies at bargain prices.

In an effort to help those unemployed by the UNO economic measures, the Chamorro government established free trade zones. These zones on the outskirts of Managua are places where foreign investors can build factories, or maquiladoras. Owners of the factories can import materials and equipment without paying a duty or tariff. Local workers assemble the materials into products that are then shipped to other nations for sale. Owners of maquiladoras pay no income or sales tax in Nicaragua and pay a minimum wage of only fourteen dollars a month to workers, according to a 2007 study by the Oregon AFL-CIO union. This is the lowest minimum wage in Central America.

The free trade zone and other neoliberal economic reforms were promoted by the World Bank, the International Monetary Fund, and the Inter-American Development Bank. With the reforms in place, the banks agreed to pardon some of the billions of dollars Nicaragua owed to them. If Chamorro refused to conform to the programs, however, the international banks would stop lending desperately needed money to the country.

Those who promote neoliberalism believe that a free market fosters social justice and peace. This is based on the theory that people living in a free market economy can work hard to become wealthy. That prevents them from pursuing criminal activities or starting revolutions. However, there were many critics of the new economic model for Nicaragua. Many of them were laid-off government workers. A 2007 article in *Envío* described the Sandinista feelings toward the free market concept:

> The idea of a state that actively participates in regulating the economy, that transfers resources from [the rich to the poor] through the socializing of medicine and basic education or the subsidizing of university education . . . is under attack. The strength of the workers who pushed the state to assume these social responsibilities is in crisis because [neoliberalism] is now granting capitalists the capacity to turn a deaf ear to union demands. . . . In neoliberalism, the idea is to return all power to the invisible hand of the market, to the law of supply and demand.

"I Felt Like a Dog"

"ONE OF THE WOMEN where I worked asked to go to the bathroom. At first the floor manager ignored her. When she asked again, he told her to wait. She insisted. It did not take her more than five minutes to return but he was furious. Three days later she was fired. The floor manager reminded us that we better learn the rules if we wanted to keep our jobs. . . .

"I hoped to make a steady income working at the maquila[dora]. . . . But I was disillusioned by the treatment of workers at the maquila. I was never hit by a manager but I saw it happen several times. They would call us stupid and lazy if we did not reach the day's quota. We could not talk to one another. I felt like a dog. After seven months, I thought, enough! I do not have much more security than before."

—Liliana, a maquiladora worker, 2000

A WOMAN MAKES SHOES AT A MAQUILADORA IN A FREE TRADE ZONE IN NICARAGUA IN 1996. THESE FACTORIES WERE ESTABLISHED AFTER CHAMORRO TOOK OFFICE. BUT WORKERS AT THE MAQUILADORAS OFTEN MADE VERY LOW WAGES.

Under that law, who wins wins and who loses loses. And who dies does so legally and legitimately. Neoliberalism's ultimate objective is for none of this to outrage or even upset us, because "that's life."

Little Change

Many Nicaraguans agreed with the Sandinista view of neoliberalism because they could see little improvement in their lives. In fact, Nicaraguans were suffering more than ever. By 1994, 54 percent of the population was unemployed. Fifty percent lived in poverty, earning no more than $2 a day. Nineteen percent lived in extreme poverty, earning less than $1 a day. The average income for Nicaraguans was $410 a year, less than one-third of what it was in the early 1980s under the Sandinistas. One in three children did not have enough to eat. Almost half of the population lacked access to safe water, and illiteracy rates were climbing. Tragically, an entire generation saw its education interrupted because of the war.

As had been the case for so long, the destiny of Nicaraguans was affected by outside forces that could not be controlled. Whether it was dictators, Marxists, or neoliberals running their government, they made it difficult for Nicaraguans to escape poverty, illiteracy, and disease.

CHAPTER 8

Fighting Corruption and Hunger

THROUGHOUT HER PRESIDENTIAL TERM, Violeta Chamorro found herself under pressure from all sides. The Sandinistas and those on the left felt that her economic policies hurt the poor. Those on the right felt that Chamorro's UNO party had made too many compromises with the Sandinistas in the National Assembly. This latter view seemed to be supported by the majority of voters in the 1994 mayoral elections. Right-wing candidates—backed by money from the United States—made gains in several major cities. In the Sandinista stronghold of Managua, many were surprised when a wealthy businessman and former Somoza official, Arnoldo Alemán, was elected mayor.

The new mayors had a powerful political ally, the United States Agency for International Development (USAID). The organization, while claiming to be nonpolitical, donated millions of dollars in aid to the new rightist administrations. Meanwhile, USAID denied funds to cities that retained Sandinista mayors. The aid was used to repair long-neglected utilities, public transportation systems, roads, and bridges.

In Managua, Alemán's popularity grew as he portrayed himself as a populist—a common man who understood the problems of the poor. In keeping with this populist image, the mayor instituted several urban renewal projects in areas still damaged from the 1972 earthquake. However, according to journalist Kevin Baxter, who lived in Nicaragua during the 1990s, Alemán "also ordered workers to whitewash dozens of the city's priceless revolutionary murals [wall paintings] and pushed the restoration of pre-insurrection names to neighborhoods and public buildings named for Sandinista martyrs."

Despite the populist claims, Alemán and the other rightist mayors had plans to bring back Somoza-style government. They even revived Somoza's discredited Liberal Party, renaming it the Liberal Alliance.

Election 1996

In 1996 the Liberal Alliance was gaining power and Daniel Ortega decided to run for president to oppose them. For his third run at the presidency, Ortega tried to modify his revolutionary image. He stopped wearing combat fatigues and softened his Marxist rhetoric. In an attempt to win over moderate voters, Ortega picked Conservative Party businessman Juan Manuel Caldera as a running mate.

The Liberal Alliance nominated Arnoldo Alemán as their candidate. There were half a dozen other political parties fielding presidential candidates too. The race was quickly narrowed down to a contest between Alemán and Ortega, however.

Like Ortega, Alemán tried to soften his image. He claimed to represent the rights and interests of ordinary citizens rather than the priorities of the rich. Journalists began to call Alemán a neopopulist. This is a term applied to leaders who claim to stand for the rights of the poor and powerless. Although neopopulists are usually from ranks of the wealthy ruling class, they use personal charm and emotional speeches to charm marginalized peasants into voting for them.

Alemán's running mate, Enrique Bolaños, was a Conservative known for his open hatred of the Sandinistas. Bolaños appealed to the weak and vulnerable by blaming their poverty on the Sandinistas.

As was typical in Nicaragua, the preelection period was chaotic and divisive. With polls giving Ortega a huge lead, Chamorro endorsed Alemán. She also said she would not turn the presidency over to Ortega if he won. Meanwhile, the Liberal Alliance pushed through a series of changes in election laws, weeks before the vote. They also insisted on changes in the membership of the Supreme Electoral Council, which oversaw the elections. According to Latin American scholar Thomas W. Walker, "[The] modifications were hard to [put into operation] on such short notice, and the changes in personnel introduced many people into the system who were inexperienced or lacking in commitment to democracy. Each step of the election was flawed by anomalies—from registration and campaigning to election-day voting and post-election vote counting."

"Nowadays, [1990s] to govern in Nicaragua means a commitment to public liberties . . . respect for all ideologies and defense of the human rights of every Nicaraguan citizen."

—Violeta Chamorro, president of Nicaragua, 1990–1996

Walker was an observer of the 1996 election. He believes that the election—the first not run by the Sandinistas since 1984—was corrupted by Liberal Alliance voting officials. Although 86 percent of the electorate voted on October 20, 1996, there were many problems counting the ballots. It took about a month for the Supreme Electoral Council to announce that Alemán received 51 percent of the vote compared to Ortega's 38 percent. The Liberals also claimed a majority of the seats in the National Assembly. Many other observers, including Jimmy Carter, believed that the election was rife with fraud. Ortega refused to concede defeat. By the time Alemán was inaugurated, only about half of the electorate believed the results were fair.

Enrique Bolaños *(left)* and Arnoldo Alemán raise their arms in victory after winning the presidential election in Nicaragua in October 1996.

"Our Children Are Watching Us"

"THE WORLD HAS BEEN exceedingly generous towards Nicaragua in these elections. The world confidently observes the consolidation of democracy in these elections. Nevertheless, the most important thing is that also our children are watching us. We must give them an example of patriotism. The Nicaraguan people are already capable of settling disagreements peacefully. Let's demonstrate that we really want to give them a better homeland."

—President Violeta Chamorro, in a speech before the National Assembly, August 20, 1996

Corruption and Scandal

Although Alemán ran as a neopopulist, after he took office in 1997, he governed as a new Somoza. According to political science professors Leslie E. Anderson and Lawrence C. Dodd, "Alemán's five-year presidency was even more clearly a government committed to the rich than Chamorro's had been, and his concentration of power in Liberal hands ostracized Conservatives as well as the Sandinistas." Alemán also tried to assume more powers than he was granted by the constitution. In addition, his party attempted to prevent Sandinistas from taking their full number of seats in the National Assembly. These maneuvers resulted in months of strikes, demonstrations, renewed armed battles, and FSLN boycotts of the assembly. Eventually Alemán was forced to back down, realizing that the Sandinistas would continue to play a role in government, even if reduced to a minority party.

Life during the Alemán Years

DURING THE 1990s, U.S. journalist Kevin Baxter lived in Managua. His 1998 article in The *Nation* magazine describes life there during the Arnoldo Alemán administration:

> [The] crushing poverty, worse now than during the final years of the Somoza regime, hasn't scared away foreign investors; U.S. companies like Motorola and Bell South, the Canadian mining firms Greenstone Resources and Triton, and large Taiwanese enterprises have all rushed in to tap one of the hemisphere's cheapest labor markets, pouring $100 million into communications, mining and hotels. . . . Indeed, the government's harsh austerity measures and slashing of social spending were enacted primarily to lure this sort of foreign investment. And the man behind the policies is Alemán, a Somoza wannabe who resembles the dictator even down to his corpulent build.
>
> But average Nicaraguans hasten to say that Alemán's much touted economic accomplishments don't trickle down to them. Nicaragua remains the hemisphere's second-poorest country . . . while per capita income is still below what it was in the late eighties. . . . No surprise, then, that recent polls found that just one in four Nicaraguans believes the country is stable politically and economically.

After settling his political problems, Alemán spent the rest of his term confronting personal scandals. In April 1998, traces of cocaine were found in the luxurious Learjet that Alemán had used as a presidential plane for about a year. The police specialist who discovered the cocaine was mysteriously murdered after news of the so-called "Narcojet" scandal was made public. Later, it was revealed that the plane had been stolen and was brought into the country with a false registration.

After the Narcojet scandal, Nicaragua's comptroller general (head of government finances), Agustín Jarquín, initiated an investigation into the president's business transactions. In February 1999, Jarquín announced that Alemán's personal fortune had inexplicably grown by 900 percent between 1990 and 1996. Alemán then threw Jarquín in jail for a month, but this did little to improve the president's image. A poll taken soon after the financial scandal broke showed that 77 percent of Nicaraguans doubted Alemán's honesty, and over 54 percent believed the Alemán administration was "more corrupt . . . [than] the notoriously corrupt Somoza government."

The Nicaraguan president was not the only person whose image suffered in the late 1990s. In April 1998, Daniel Ortega's thirty-eight-year-old stepdaughter, Zoilamerica Narvaez, accused him of sexually abusing her for more than twenty years, starting when she was an adolescent. Sandinista officials denounced these charges as politically motivated, but Ortega never denied them.

Accusations against Ortega and Alemán hurt their respective political parties. Public support for both the Liberal Alliance and the FSLN dropped by as much as 20 percentage points.

Hurricane Mitch Hammers Nicaragua

In October 1998, the deadliest Atlantic hurricane since 1780 hit Nicaragua. Hurricane Mitch brought winds of 180 miles (290 km) per hour and dumped 50 inches (127 centimeters) of rain in some areas. The hurricane directly affected 2 million people, about two-thirds of the population, and killed about 3,000 people. The Category 5 "monster" hurricane destroyed 23,900 houses and damaged 17,600 more. At least 368,300 people were left homeless—about 20 percent of the population. Mitch also destroyed 340 schools and 90 health centers. Economic damages totaled $1.5 billion.

The damage from Hurricane Mitch was more widespread than that of the Christmas Earthquake of 1972, which was centered in Managua. And as had happened under Somoza, Alemán used the disaster relief to further his political ambitions. The Liberal Party took charge of most aid distribution, and areas with elected Sandinista officials were denied relief. The president, who openly expressed hatred of Castro, also refused to allow Cuban doctors into the country to help with the growing public health crises. Alemán even refused to declare a state of national emergency, saying, "Such a mobilization would be something that the Sandinistas would do—and [I'm] certainly . . . no Sandinista."

A WOMAN AND HER CHILD SIT ON THE REMAINS OF THEIR HOUSE IN NORTHWESTERN NICARAGUA AFTER HURRICANE MITCH HIT IN OCTOBER 1998.

In the wake of Hurricane Mitch, Alemán was severely criticized and his popularity continued to diminish. This forced him, ironically, to make concessions with another unpopular figure, his archrival Daniel Ortega. Together Alemán and Ortega made deals that would only benefit the interests of their parties. The men worked out deals to pack the Supreme Court, the Supreme Electoral Council, and the comptroller general's office with supporters. Alemán would no longer be bothered by investigations of his business practices. And through this maneuvering, Ortega would be in a stronger position when he ran for president once again in 2001.

"A Friend to Terrorists"

In the first election of the twenty-first century, it seemed as if Nicaragua had returned to the Somoza era. The Sandinistas were constantly discredited in the media. The powerful members of the Liberal Alliance were concentrating ever more wealth into the hands of a few. Statistics showed that 45 percent of all income in Nicaragua was going to the richest 10 percent of the population, while only 14 percent went to the large majority living in poverty. And as had happened throughout the twentieth century, the United States was heavily involved in another Nicaraguan election. When Ortega showed a seven-point lead over the Liberal Alliance candidate, Vice President Bolaños, the United States applied pressure on the Conservative candidate to drop out so the anti-Sandinista vote would not be split.

As in previous years, the Nicaraguan election was influenced by events thousands of miles away. After the September 11, 2001, terrorist attacks on the World Trade Center and the Pentagon, U.S. officials began to link Ortega to terrorism. To enforce this message, the

United States donated millions of dollars to the Bolaños campaign. The campaign was advised to use the terrorist theme in their campaign literature. Enormous signs hung along the streets in Managua proclaiming: "NICARAGUA DOES NOT WANT A PRESIDENT WHO IS A FRIEND TO TERRORISTS." Author Phyllis Ponvert, who lived in Nicaragua, describes how the Bolaños television campaign ads used the same ideas: "Pro-Bolaños ads . . . showed images of Saddam Hussein, Libya's Moammar Gadhafi, Fidel Castro, and finally, Osama bin Laden. Then the image faded into Daniel Ortega in a military uniform. This was meant to . . . insinuate that Ortega shared responsibility for the attacks on New York and Washington!"

The campaign worked. Bolaños won by a fourteen-point margin over Ortega. However, after the election, former president Carter condemned the role played by the United States: "I personally disapprove of statements or actions by any country that might tend to influence the vote of people in another sovereign nation."

"You Stole the People's Trust"

As Nicaragua entered a new century, the situation for the average citizen was little changed. The neoliberal reforms put in place by Chamorro and Alemán did not erase Nicaragua's problems. Bridges, roads, and buildings damaged by Hurricane Mitch remained in ruins. The majority of Nicaraguans continued to live in dire poverty without adequate food, education, health care, or housing. The Sandinista party, which once provided hope, was now simply a vehicle for Ortega's personal ambitions.

With an overwhelming array of problems, the seventy-year-old Bolaños raised few hopes. Alemán had set himself up as a major power by retaining a position in the National Assembly. Many feared the former president would continue to rule from behind the scenes. The new president, however, refused to allow this to happen. In August 2002, Bolaños accused Alemán and thirteen others of stealing $100 million in public funds and diverting the money to secret bank accounts in Panama. When announcing the theft, Bolaños stated, "Arnoldo, I never dreamed you would betray your people like this. You took the pensions of retirees, medicine from the sick, [and] salaries from the teachers. You stole the people's trust."

Alemán was stripped of his leadership position in the National Assembly and put on trial. On December 7, 2003, the former president was sentenced to twenty years in prison on dozens of charges including money laundering, embezzlement, and corruption. Because of health problems, Alemán was allowed to serve his sentence under house arrest, a form of legal confinement in which he was not allowed to leave his home.

Ortega Is President—Again

By the time Alemán was convicted, Nicaraguans had lived through more than a decade of economic reforms that lowered inflation and attracted major corporations to Nicaragua. Still, according to Anderson and Dodd, "The mass of citizens faced substantial personal reversal and family hardship during these years, and the nation at large suffered as a result of the corruption of Alemán and his cronies."

By 2005, more than a quarter century since he first took power, Daniel Ortega decided to run for president once again. By this time, however, there was open rebellion within the ranks of the Sandinista Party. The sixty-year-old Ortega was criticized for compromising his ideals when he worked with Alemán to retain political power. Ortega was also under fire for keeping tight control over the FSLN, expelling members who challenged his leadership.

Although Sandinista political insiders had problems with Ortega, many Nicaraguan peasants treated him as a celebrity. Wherever he appeared, the Sandinista leader was hugged and kissed by supporters who chanted his name and waved black and red Sandinista flags. Ortega aides doled out small stipends to needy people from party funds. These gifts, worth five or ten dollars, were used by peasants to buy clothes, schoolbooks, food, and other necessities. And Ortega continued to give fiery anti-U.S. speeches, such as the one in El Jicaral in September 2005 where he stated: "The U.S. no longer rules Latin America! The Yankees no longer rule Nicaragua! . . . The triumph of the Sandinistas will raise the morale of Latin America. . . . Other countries will say—'look, that small country got away with it—so can we! We will spread the revolution.'"

Presidential candidate Daniel Ortega greets children as he campaigns in October 2006.

As Ortega repeated rhetoric from decades passed, so too did leaders in Washington. Former Reagan and George H. W. Bush speechwriter Mark Klugmann wrote in the *National Review*, "A Nicaragua that opens its arms to murderous radicalism poses a threat for America and the world. . . . A nuclear North Korea and a nuclear Iran could be in position, with an ally so close to our porous frontier, to wreak the havoc we once thought only the Soviet Union could ever bring home."

Ironically, such criticism only helped to solidify Ortega's support. According to Carlos Fernando Chamorro, Violeta's son and a former editor of the Sandinista newspaper *Barricada*, "Every time Washington attacks Ortega, his supporters close ranks."

On November 6, 2006, despite threats that U.S. officials would cut off $850 million in aid to Nicaragua, Ortega won 39 percent of the vote. His opponent, banker Eduardo Montealegre of the Liberal Alliance, won only 31 percent. In the five-way race for the presidency, the margin was enough to hand a victory to Ortega's Sandinista-led coalition. The FSLN also took a majority of seats in the National Assembly. After his victory, Ortega stated that his government would construct a new economic, social, and political model to free Nicaragua from the international institutions and set up a "direct democracy" in which the "people are the President."

"A guerrilla who rose to power, then lost it, relinquishing it peacefully in 1990 . . . many of his adversaries and former fighting colleagues think that [Daniel] Ortega deserves the opportunity to govern again."

—Raúl Arévalo, in *La Jornada*, 2006

The Zero Hunger Program

When Ortega was inaugurated for a second time in 2007, it seemed as if the FSLN had been redeemed. Countless impartial studies concluded that despite the Contra war, most Nicaraguans were better off during the Sandinista regime. In 2007 Ortega was free to wage a new war, this time against hunger. One of his first acts as president was to institute the Zero Hunger Program with $50 million in funds freed up after the Inter-American Development Bank canceled Nicaragua's debt. The objective of the Zero Hunger Program is to eliminate extreme poverty and reduce hunger. Another $100 million for this difficult effort is to be provided by the United Nations World Food Program. Venezuelan president Hugo Chavez has promised to add $300 million a year.

Between 2007 and 2012, the Sandinistas plan to deliver two thousand dollars in supplies to about seventy-five thousand rural families, most of whom earn less than five hundred dollars a year. The supplies will consist of a pregnant cow and a pregnant sow, five chickens and a rooster, seeds, fruit-bearing plants, and plants for reforestation. Families will use these items to provide milk, meat, eggs, fruits, vegetables, and cereals for themselves. The hope is that over time, extra food will be produced. This can be sold at local markets and used for export. The families that benefit from the project will be required to pay back 20 percent of the amount that they receive in order to create a rural fund that will guarantee the continuity of the program.

In the End

Three decades after the end of the oppressive Samoza regime, most Nicaraguans continue to live with hunger and poverty. Their situation

Promoting the Natural World

IN THE TWENTY-FIRST CENTURY, a majority of Nicaraguans continue to struggle from day to day. However, an unexpected segment of the economy has experienced growth beyond all expectations. Nicaragua has become known as a nature lover's paradise, and the number of tourists visiting the nation has been growing by 20 percent a year since 2005. This has been attributed to the seventy-six parks and protected nature areas that cover nearly one-fifth of Nicaragua's landmass. These areas include lakes, volcanoes, and the largest area of untouched rain forest north of the Amazon. Nicaragua is also home to endangered species such as jaguars, and howler, white-faced, and spider monkeys. Other attractions include rare jungle birds, butterflies, and orchids. While Nicaragua retains a negative image from the Contra war years, the nation has been at peace since 1990. Because of its friendly people and stable government, according to the U.S. State Department, Nicaragua is the safest country for tourists in Central America.

did improve temporarily in the aftermath of the Sandinista revolution. However, it is impossible to know how the Sandinista government would have continued to perform if it had not had violent opposition from the U.S.-led Contras. Some argue that the nation was quickly becoming a repressive Communist regime like Cuba. Others believe that with the collapse of Communism, Sandinista politics would have moderated. Aspects of free market capitalism would have been put in place to finance Sandinista social programs. Whatever the case, the people of Nicaragua today enjoy freedom of speech, a free press, and democratic elections. Though the country continues to rebuild from generations of upheaval and repression, these freedoms would not exist if the nation had remained under a Somoza-like dictatorship.

Timeline

1821 The Republic of Nicaragua is founded.

1909 On November 18, U.S. warships are sent to Nicaragua to protect U.S. business interests.

1912 U.S. Marines occupy Nicaragua to quell civilian unrest.

1925 U.S. forces withdraw from Nicaragua, and the Constitutionalist War begins.

1926 U.S. Marines return to Nicaragua to stop the Constitutionalist War and fight nationalist guerrillas led by Commander Augusto Sandino.

1933 On January 1, the U.S. Marines pull out of Nicaragua. The United States appoints Nicaraguan military officer Anastasio Somoza as commander of the National Guard.

1934 Somoza has Augusto Sandino assassinated on February 21.

1936 On June 6, Anastasio Somoza leads a coup against Nicaraguan president Juan Bautista Sacasa.

1937 Somoza has himself elected president of Nicaragua on January 1 and establishes a dictatorship.

1947 Anastasio Somoza Debayle is appointed chief director of the National Guard by his father President Somoza.

1956 On September 21, President Somoza is shot four times by assassin Rigoberto López Pérez. Somoza dies four days later. He is succeeded by his son Luis Somoza Debayle on September 25.

1959 Fidel Castro deposes dictator Fulgencio Batista in Cuba on January 1.

Carlos Fonseca Amador forms the National Liberation Front, known by its Spanish acronym FLN.

1963 “Sandinista” is added to the FLN’s name, creating the Frente Sandinista de Liberación Nacional, or FSLN.

1967 Anastasio Somoza Debayle makes himself president of Nicaragua on February 5.

1972 The Christmas Earthquake of December 23 strikes Managua, leveling six hundred square blocks and killing twenty thousand.

1974 In December fifteen FSLN guerrillas invade the home of the minister of agriculture and hold several leading Nicaraguan officials hostage.

1978 On January 10, Pedro Joaquín Chamorro, editor in chief of *La Prensa*, is murdered by assassins working for Somoza. Riots break out in several cities, and a general strike shuts down the entire country for ten days. On August 22, Sandinistas seize the National Legislative Palace, take more than one thousand hostages, and demand a $500,000 ransom. In September the FSLN coordinates a countrywide uprising known as the September insurrection, which is brutally put down by the National Guard.

1979 After fifty-two days of fighting, the FSLN forces Somoza to resign, July 8. On July 19, the Sandinista revolution concludes as the National Guard dissolves and FSLN fighters take over the National Palace.

1980 Ronald Reagan is elected president of the United States.

1981 On March 9, Reagan gives the CIA $19.5 million to form a proxy army to wage a low-intensity conflict in Nicaragua.

In September FSLN leader Daniel Ortega declares a state of economic and social emergency.

1982 The Contra war begins.

1984 In January the CIA mines three Nicaragua harbors. In October the U.S. Congress suspends all aid to the Contras. In November Ortega is elected president of Nicaragua. Reagan is reelected U.S. president.

1985 In March Reagan imposes a trade embargo against Nicaragua. In November U.S. National Security Council employee Oliver North sells missiles to Iran to raise money for the Contras.

1986 The U.S. Congress authorizes $100 million in aid for the Contras in June. On October 5, Sandinistas shoot down a Contra supply plane with an American, Eugene Hasenfus, aboard. In November North's missile sale to Iran is revealed, sparking a congressional investigation into the Iran-Contra affair.

1988 The Arias Peace Plan ends the Contra war on March 23.

1990 On April 25, Violeta Chamorro is inaugurated president of Nicaragua, ending more than ten years of Sandinista rule.

1996 Former Somoza official Arnoldo Alemán is elected president of Nicaragua.

1998 On October 29, Hurricane Mitch strikes Nicaragua, killing at least three thousand people and causing $1.5 billion in damages.

2003 Arnoldo Alemán is sentenced to twenty years in prison on dozens of charges on December 7.

2006 On November 6, Daniel Ortega is elected president for a second time, after being out of office for fifteen years.

2008 In May President Ortega holds a Latin and Central American summit meeting in Managua to discuss plans to deal with the food crisis facing the region due to high oil prices and crop shortages. In June Ortega appoints Rosario Murillo head of the social cabinet, putting her in charge of all government social programs including Zero Hunger and the National Social Welfare System.

Glossary

agribusiness: a large-scale farming operation run by a major corporation

capitalism: an economic system where people are motivated by profit and are free to compete with one another with limited government regulation

clandestine: secret, or covert

collective: a farm or business run by its workers with guidance from the government

Communism: a political system where all members of society share a nation's property and wealth

counterrevolutionary: a person who opposes a revolution. In Nicaragua counterrevolutionaries who opposed the Sandinistas were called Contras.

coup: overthrow of the government

demobilization: the act of discharging personnel from armed forces and sending them home after a war

guerrilla: a member of a paramilitary force whose goal is to overthrow a government

imperialism: a system in which a powerful country extends economic, military, and political control over less powerful countries

junta: a ruling council or legislative body within the government

Marxism: a political philosophy devised by Karl Marx in which average workers, or the proletariat, control the means of production. In this system, no single class of persons is more important than any other.

paramilitary: describing an organization modeled on the military, organized to fight within a country against an official ruling power

propaganda: information produced by a government or political organization meant to promote policies, philosophy, ideas, and causes

sympathizer: someone who shares the ideals of another political group

Who's Who?

Pedro Joaquín Chamorro (1924–1978) was the owner and editor in chief of *La Prensa*, the Managua newspaper that acted as a leading voice against the Somoza regime. Chamorro began working for his family-owned newspaper in 1948 and became editor in 1952. As a strong opponent of Somoza, Chamorro was jailed and tortured several times for writing and publishing articles critical of the government. In 1960 he was jailed for nine years for treason. After his release, *La Prensa* became the main platform for the opposition. Although Chamorro was a member of the rightist Conservative Party and opposed the Marxist philosophies of the Sandinistas, he supported their efforts to overthrow Somoza. Chamorro was killed by gunmen who opened fire on his car with machine guns. His murder sparked the Sandinista revolution after an estimated thirty thousand people rioted in the streets of Managua.

Violeta Barrios de Chamorro (b. 1929) was the forty-eighth president of Nicaragua, from April 1990 to January 1997, and the first and only woman so far to hold that office. Chamorro was born to a wealthy family and educated in the United States. Married to Pedro Joaquín Chamorro, she took over editorship of *La Prensa* when her husband was assassinated in 1978. After the Sandinista revolution, Chamorro became a member of the Junta of National Reconstruction that replaced the Somoza government. She resigned in April 1980 because of sharp political differences with the Sandinistas. After her resignation, she used *La Prensa* as a platform to criticize the FSLN and Daniel Ortega. In 1990 Chamorro was elected president. During her term, she instituted neoliberal economic reforms that reversed many Sandinista policies.

Carlos Fonseca Amador (1936–1976) was a teacher and founder of the Sandinista National Liberation Front (FSLN). His father was a member of a wealthy family, and his mother was a peasant. Fonseca studied Marxism in high school and became a student activist in college, traveling to the Soviet Union in 1957 to attend a Communist youth gathering. He founded the

FSLN in 1959, taking inspiration from the revolution in Cuba led by Fidel Castro. Fonseca was killed in the mountains of Nicaragua, three years before the FSLN overthrew the Somoza dynasty.

Oliver North (b. 1943) was a lieutenant colonel in the U.S. Marines. He was implicated as the architect of the Iran-Contra affair in 1986. He began his military career in Vietnam and was awarded the Silver Star, Bronze Star, and two Purple Heart medals. While working for the National Security Council, North was involved in the clandestine sale of weapons to Iran, an act that violated several federal laws. Millions of dollars from the weapons sale were diverted to the Contras. When the affair was discovered, North illegally shredded thousands of pages of documents concerning the sale. He was indicted on sixteen felony counts in 1988 and was convicted of three in 1989. Although he was sentenced to three years in prison, North's conviction was thrown out on a legal technicality.

Daniel Ortega Saavedra (b. 1945) was head of Nicaragua's five-person Junta of National Reconstruction. This group ruled Nicaragua after the Sandinistas won the revolution in 1979. Ortega was born to middle-class parents who opposed the Somoza regime, and he was first arrested for his political activities when he was fifteen. He attended the Universidad Centroamericana in Managua, where he joined the FSLN in 1963. After taking power, Ortega served as Nicaragua's acting president until he was officially elected to a six-year term in 1984. Although his term ended in 1990, Ortega ran for president two more times and won reelection in 2006.

Ronald Reagan (1911–2004) was the fortieth president of the United States from 1981 to 1989. He implemented the Reagan Doctrine, a political strategy that opposed the global influence of Marxism and Communism in developing nations. Reagan saw Nicaragua as a testing ground for the doctrine after the Sandinistas installed a Marxist government and began working with the Soviet Union, Cuba, and other Communist governments. To counter these influences, Reagan authorized the Central Intelligence Agency to fund the Contra army in order to topple the Sandinista regime.

Augusto César Sandino (1895–1934) was a Nicaraguan revolutionary. His father was a prominent landowner, and his mother was an Indian peasant who worked on his father's estate. Sandino became an activist as a young man after working under extremely harsh conditions in a U.S.-owned gold mine. Between 1927 and 1933, Sandino led a rebellion against the U.S. military presence in Nicaragua. He was assassinated by men working for Anastasio Somoza García. Sandino's legacy inspired revolutionaries in the Sandinista National Liberation Front (FSLN).

Anastasio "Tachito" Somoza Debayle (1925–1980) was the president of Nicaragua from May 1, 1967, to May 1, 1972, and from December 1, 1974, to July 17, 1979. However, as head of the National Guard, he was the unchallenged ruler of the country from 1967 to 1979. Somoza was widely considered a brutal dictator who made a personal fortune by looting the Nicaraguan economy. After being overthrown by the Sandinistas in 1979, he was assassinated in Paraguay in 1980.

Luis Somoza Debayle (1922–1967) became the fortieth president of Nicaragua in 1956 upon the death of his father, Anastasio Somoza García. He ruled until 1967, when his brother, Anastasio Somoza Debayle, was made president in a rigged election. Several months later, Luis Somoza died suddenly following a heart attack.

Anastasio "Tacho" Somoza García (1896–1956) was the thirty-fourth and thirty-ninth president of Nicaragua. However, he ruled as a dictator continuously from 1936 until 1956. Somoza was the son of a wealthy coffee planter. He went to college in Pennsylvania, where he learned to speak perfect English. After marrying Salvadora Debayle Sacasa, a member of one of Nicaragua's wealthiest families, Somoza served as Nicaragua's minister of war and minister of foreign relations. He became chief director of the National Guard in 1933 before becoming president three years later in a coup. Somoza was shot four times by a twenty-seven–year-old poet, Rigoberto López Pérez. Somoza died four days later on September 25, 1956.

Source Notes

4 Lawrence Pezzullo and Ralph Pezzullo, *At the Fall of Somoza.* (Pittsburgh: University of Pittsburgh Press, 1993), 228.

5 Stephen Kinzer, *Blood of Brothers* (New York: G. P. Putnam's Sons, 1991), 72.

6 Ibid., 73.

7 John A. Booth, *The End and the Beginning: The Nicaraguan Revolution* (Boulder, CO: Westview Press, 1982), 11.

11 Richard Millet, *Guardians of the Dynasty* (Maryknoll, NY: Orbis Books, 1977), 52.

12 Tony Jenkins, *Nicaragua and the United States* (New York: Franklin Watts, 1989), 33.

13 Ibid., 37.

13 George Black, *Triumph of the People* (London: Zed Press, 1981), 20.

17 Eduardo Crawley, *Nicaragua in Perspective* (New York: St. Martin's Press, 1984), 116.

17 Jenkins, *Nicaragua and the United States*, 53.

18 Matilde Zimmerman, *Sandinista Carlos Fonseca and the Nicaraguan Revolution* (Durham, NC: Duke University Press, 2000), 50.

18 Ernesto "Che" Guevara, "Guerilla Warfare," *North Carolina State University*, August 28, 2005, http://social.chass.ncsu.edu/slatta/hi216/documents/che.htm#11 (August 21, 2008).

22 Booth, *The End and the Beginning*, 141.

24 Jay Mallin, "The Great Managua Earthquake," *Geoscience Institution of Nicaragua*, April 11, 2007, http://www.ineter.gob.ni/geofisica/sis/managua72/mallin/great01.html (August 22, 2008).

25 Black, *Triumph of the People*, 59.

27 Bernard Diederich, *Somoza* (New York: E. F. Dutton, 1981), 111.

27 Ibid., 113.

29 University of Pittsburgh, "The Somoza Dynasty," *University Center for International Studies*, 2006, http://www.ucis.pitt.edu/clas/nicaragua_proj/history/somoza/Hist-Somoza-dinasty.pdf (August 21, 2008).

30 Thomas W. Walker, *Nicaragua: Living in the Shadow of the Eagle* (Boulder, CO: Westview Press, 2003), 35.

32 Bianca Jagger, "Diary," *New Statesman*, June 28, 2004, http://www.newstatesman.com/200406280003 (August 21, 2008).

33 Black, *Triumph of the People*, 129–130.

37 Ibid., 180.

38 Kinzer, *Blood of Brothers*, 74.

41 CNN, "Interviews: Daniel Ortega," *CNN Cold War: Episode 18*, 1998, http://www.cnn.com/SPECIALS/cold.war/episodes/18/interviews/ortega (August 21, 2008).

42 Kinzer, *Blood of Brothers*, 78.

43 Frances Moore Lappé and Joseph Collins, *Now We Can Speak* (San Francisco: Institute for Food and Development Policy, 1982), 22.

45 Ibid., 21–22.

47 Lynn Horton, *Peasants in Arms* (Athens, OH: Center for International Studies, 1998), 106.

47 CNN, "Interviews: Oscar Manuel Sobalvarro," *CNN Cold War: Episode 18*, 1998, http://www.cnn.com/SPECIALS/cold.war/episodes/18/interviews/sobalvarro (August 21, 2008).

48 Lappé and Collins, *Now We Can Speak*, 31.

48 Thomas Walker, ed., *Nicaragua: The First Five Years* (New York: Praeger, 1985), 49.

51 Margaret Randall, *Sandino's Daughter Revisited* (New Brunswick, NJ: Rutgers University Press, 1994), 34.

52–53 Ibid., 244–245.

54 Thomas W. Walker, ed., *Revolution & Counterrevolution in Nicaragua.* (Boulder, CO: Westview Press, 1992), 323.

55 David Ryan, *U.S.-Sandinista Diplomatic Relations* (New York: St. Martin's Press, 1995), 8.

56 Kinzer, *Blood of Brothers*, 79.

57 Shirley Christian, *Nicaragua: Revolution in the Family* (New York: Random House, 1985), 124.

57–58 Ibid., 171.

58 Ibid., 175.

59 U.S. Department of State, "Reagan Doctrine, 1985," *USA.gov*, December 20, 2007, http://www.state.gov/r/pa/ho/time/rd/17741.htm (August 22, 2008).

60 Walker, *Revolution & Counterrevolution in Nicaragua*, 325.

60 Ibid.

61 Robert Kagan, *A Twilight Struggle* (New York: Free Press), 168.

62 Walker, *Revolution & Counterrevolution in Nicaragua*, 326.

62 Jack Nelson-Pallmeyer, "War Against the Poor: Low-Intensity Conflict and Christian Faith," *Religion On-Line*, 2008, http://www.religion-online.org/showchapter.asp?title=2288&C=2186 (August 21, 2008).

64 Walker, *Revolution & Counterrevolution in Nicaragua*, 331.

65 Edgar Chamorro, *Packaging the Contras: A Case of CIA Disinformation* (New York: Institute for Media Analysis, 1987), 49.

67–68 Envío Digital, "Halcón Vista and the Response of the Nicaraguan People," *Central American University*, November 1981, http://www.envio.org.ni/articulo/3122 (August 21, 2008).

68 Envío Digital, "The Silent Invasion," *Central American University*, August 1982, http://www.envio.org.ni/articulo/3371 (August 21, 2008).

70 GigFoot, "Did You Know?" *GigFoot Webchat*, 2007, http://www.gigfoot.net/lol/facts/3755.html (December 2007).

71 Walker, *Revolution & Counterrevolution in Nicaragua*, 329.

74 Roy Gutman, *Banana Diplomacy* (New York: Simon and Schuster, 1988), 151.

74–75 Richard Araujo, "The Sandinista War on Human Rights," *Heritage Foundation*, July 19, 1983, http://www.heritage.org/Research/LatinAmerica/bg277.cfm (August 21, 2008).

75 Human Rights Watch, "Nicaragua," *hrw.org*, 2006, http://www.hrw.org/reports/1989/WR89/Nicaragu.htm (August 21, 2008).

75 William M. Leogrande, *Our Own Backyard* (Chapel Hill: University of North Carolina, 1998), 414.

75–76 Peter Rosset and John Vandermeer, eds., *Nicaragua: Unfinished Revolution* (New York: Grove Press, 1986), 227.

76 Thomas W. Walker, ed., *Reagan Versus the Sandinistas* (Boulder, CO: Westview Press, 1987), 255.

76 Leogrande, *Our Own Backyard*, 413.

78 Peter Davis, *Where Is Nicaragua?* (New York: Simon and Schuster, 1987), 271–272.

78 Franklin Foer, "Founding Fakers," *New Republic*, August 18, 2003, available online at *Gene Expression*, n.d., http://www.gnxp.com/MT2/archives/000857.html (August 21, 2008).

78 Leogrande, *Our Own Backyard*, 331.

80 Ibid., 332.

80 Ibid., 330.

81 Middlebury College, "International Law PSCI 0236," *Segue*, n.d., https://segue.middlebury.edu/index.php?action=site&site=psci0236a-f06 (August 21, 2008).

81 Leogrande, *Our Own Backyard*, 334.

82 Marlene Dixon, ed., *On Trial: Reagan's War Against Nicaragua* (San Francisco: Synthesis Publications, 1985), 230–231.

82 Leogrande, *Our Own Backyard*, 344.

83 Walker, *Nicaragua: Living in the Shadow*, 151.

84 Kagan, *A Twilight Struggle*, 319.

84 Walker, *Nicaragua: Living in the Shadow*, 157.

86 Bernard Gwertzman, "Reagan Aide Says Contras Can Fell Sandinistas," *New York Times*, 2007, http://query.nytimes.com/gst/fullpage.html?res=940DEEDF103DF93AA35752C0A961948260&sec=&spon=&pagewanted=all (August 22, 2008).

87 Oliver North, "Oliver North Quotes," *Brainyquote*, 2007, http://www.brainyquote.com/quotes/authors/o/oliver_north.html (August 22, 2008).

87 Ronald Reagan, "Creators of the Future," *Conservative Political Action Committee*, 2006, http://www.conservative.org/pressroom/reagan/reagan1985.asp (August 22, 2008).

89 Holly Sklar, *Washington's War on Nicaragua* (Boston: South End Press, 1988), 266.

91 Walker, *Reagan Versus the Sandinistas*, 256.

91 Roger Miranda and William Ratliff, *The Civil War in Nicaragua* (New Brunswick, NJ: Transaction Publishers, 1993), 241.

93 Peter Ford, "Nicaragua: A Siren to Many Foreigners," *Christian Science Monitor*, June 12, 1986, 7.

94 Walker, *Reagan Versus the Sandinistas*, 260.

94 Sklar, *Washington's War on Nicaragua*, 265.

95 Ibid., 268.

97 Envío Digital, "Hasenfus: Nothing but the Fact," *Central American University*, November 1986, http://www.envio.org.ni/articulo/3243 (August 22, 2008).

97 Miranda and Ratliff, *The Civil War in Nicaragua*, 244.

100 Walker, *Nicaragua: Living in the Shadow*, 56.

106 Sergio de Castro, ed., *Elections 90* (San Francisco: Barricada USA, 1990), 46.

107 Leogrande, *Our Own Backyard*, 558.

109 Ibid., 562.

109–110 Ilja A. Luciak, *The Sandinista Legacy* (Gainesville: University Press of Florida, 1995), 183.

110 Ibid.

110 Cynthia Chavez Metoyer, *Women and the State in Post-Sandinista Nicaragua* (Boulder, CO: Lynne Rienner Publishers, 2000), 50.

112 Ibid., 52.

113 Walker, *Nicaragua: Living in the Shadow*, 196.

116–118 Envío Digital, "Has a Neoliberal Democracy Been Institutionalized in Nicaragua?" *Central American University*, July 2006, http://www.envio.org.ni/articulo/3326 (August 22, 2008).

117 Metoyer, *Women and the State in Post-Sandinista Nicaragua*, 84.

120 Kevin Baxter, "Under the Volcano: Neoliberalism Finds Nicaragua," *Third World Traveler*, April 6, 1998, http:// www.thirdworldtraveler.com/New_World_Order/Under_Volcano.html (August 22, 2008).

121 Walker, *Nicaragua: Living in the Shadow*, 62.

121 Leslie E. Anderson and Lawrence C. Dodd, *Learning Democracy* (Chicago: University of Chicago Press, 2005), 225.

123 Ibid.

123 Ibid., 232.

124 Baxter, "Under the Volcano."

125 Envío Digital "The Comptroller's Office and Corruption: What Does Managua Think?" *Central American University*, April 1999, http://www.envio.org.ni/articulo/2239 (August 22, 2008).

126 Alejandro Bendaña, "The Politics of Hurricane Mitch in Nicaragua," *Parkland Institute*, Winter 1999, http://www.ualberta.ca/PARKLAND/post/Vol-III-No1/05bendana.html (August 22, 2008).

128 Phyllis Ponvert, "Nicaragua Elections, American Style," *University of Michigan*, December 2001–January 2002, http://www-personal.umich.edu/~lormand/agenda/0112/nicaragua.htm (August 22, 2008).

128 Ibid.

128 Walker, *Nicaragua: Living in the Shadow*, 68.

129 Gioconda Belli, "Nicaragua; a Crusader Looks to the U.S.," *Los Angeles Times*, September 8, 2002, M2.

129 Anderson and Dodd, *Learning Democracy*, 247.

130 Danna Harman, "Remember Daniel Ortega? He's Back," *Christian Science Monitor*, September 15, 2005, http://www.csmonitor.com/2005/0915/p01s04-woam.html (August 22, 2008).

131 Mark Engler, "The Return of Daniel Ortega," *Nation*, November 7, 2006, http://www.thenation.com/doc/20061120/ortega (August 22, 2008).

131 Harman, "Remember Daniel Ortega? He's Back."

131 Envío Digital, "Where Are We Heading?" *Central American University*, May 2007, http://www.envio.org.ni/articulo/3554 (August 22, 2008).

131 BBC, "Press Wary about Ortega Victory," *BBC News*, November 8, 2006, http://news.bbc.co.uk/1/hi/world/americas/6128310.stm (August 22, 2008).

Selected Bibliography

Anderson, Leslie E., and Lawrence C. Dodd. *Learning Democracy.* Chicago: University of Chicago Press, 2005.

Araujo, Richard. "The Sandinista War on Human Rights." *Heritage Foundation.* July 19, 1983. http://www.heritage.org/Research/LatinAmerica/bg277.cfm (August 22, 2008).

Baxter, Kevin. "Under the Volcano: Neoliberalism Finds Nicaragua." *Third World Traveler.* April 6, 1998. http://www.thirdworldtraveler.com/New_World_Order/Under_Volcano.html (August 22, 2008).

Belli, Gioconda. "Nicaragua; a Crusader Looks to the U.S." *Los Angeles Times,* September 8, 2002, M2.

Bendaña, Alejandro. "The Politics of Hurricane Mitch in Nicaragua." *Parkland Institute.* Winter 1999. http://www.ualberta.ca/PARKLAND/post/Vol-III-No1/05bendana.html (August 22, 2008).

Black, George. *Triumph of the People.* London: Zed Press, 1981.

Booth, John A. *The End and the Beginning: The Nicaraguan Revolution.* Boulder, CO: Westview Press, 1982.

Chamorro, Edgar. *Packaging the Contras: A Case of CIA Disinformation.* New York: Institute for Media Analysis, 1987.

Christian, Shirley. *Nicaragua: Revolution in the Family.* New York: Random House, 1985.

Crawley, Eduardo. *Nicaragua in Perspective.* New York: St. Martin's Press, 1984.

Davis, Peter. *Where Is Nicaragua?* New York: Simon and Schuster, 1987.

Diederich, Bernard. *Somoza.* New York: E. F. Dutton, 1981.

Dowd, Maureen. "McFarlane and North: The Fatherly Touch." *New York Times.* May 12, 1987. http://query.nytimes.com/gst/fullpage.html?res=9B0DE3DC1139F931A25756C0A961948260 (August 22, 2008).

Engler, Mark. "The Return of Daniel Ortega." *Nation.* November 7, 2006. http://www.thenation.com/doc/20061120/ortega (August 22, 2008).

Envío Digital. "The Comptroller's Office and Corruption: What Does Managua Think?" *Central American University.* April 1999. http://www.envio.org.ni/articulo/2239 (August 22, 2008).

———. "Halcón Vista and the Response of the Nicaraguan People." *Central American University.* November 1981. http://www.envio.org.ni/articulo/3122 (August 22, 2008).

———. "Has a Neoliberal Democracy Been Institutionalized in Nicaragua?" *Central American University*, July 2006. http://www.envio.org.ni/articulo/3326 (August 22, 2008).

———. "Where Are We Heading?" *Central American University.* May 2007. http://www.envio.org.ni/articulo/3554 (August 22, 2008).

Ford, Peter. "Nicaragua: A Siren to Many Foreigners," *Christian Science Monitor*, June 12, 1986.

GigFoot. "Did You Know?" *GigFoot Webchat.* 2007. http://www.gigfoot.net/lol/facts/3755.html (December 2007).

Goodman, Amy. "Noam Chomsky on Reagan's Legacy." *Democracy Now.* June 7, 2004. http://www.democracynow.org/2004/6/7/noam_chomsky_on_reagans_legacy_bush (August 22, 2008).

Gutman, Roy. *Banana Diplomacy.* New York: Simon and Schuster, 1988.

Gwertzman, Bernard. "Reagan Aide Says Contras Can Fell Sandinistas." *New York Times.* January 9, 1987. http://query.nytimes.com/gst/fullpage.html?res=940DEEDF103DF93AA35752C0A961948260&sec=&spon=&pagewanted=all (August 22, 2008).

Horton, Lynn. *Peasants in Arms.* Athens, OH: Center for International Studies, 1998.

Human Rights Watch. "Nicaragua." *hrw.org*. 2006. http://www.hrw.org/reports/1989/WR89/Nicaragu.htm (August 22, 2008).

Jenkins, Tony. *Nicaragua and the United States*. New York: Franklin Watts, 1989.

Kagan, Robert. *A Twilight Struggle*. New York: Free Press, 1996.

Kinzer, Stephen. *Blood of Brothers*. New York: G. P. Putnam's Sons, 1991.

Lappé, Frances Moore, and Joseph Collins. *Now We Can Speak*. San Francisco: Institute for Food and Development Policy, 1982.

Leogrande, William M. *Our Own Backyard*. Chapel Hill: University of North Carolina, 1998.

Luciak, Ilja A. *The Sandinista Legacy*. Gainesville: University Press of Florida, 1995.

Metoyer, Cynthia Chavez. *Women and the State in Post-Sandinista Nicaragua*. Boulder, CO: Lynne Rienner Publishers, 2000.

Middlebury College. "International Law PSCI 0236." *Segue*. N.d. https://segue.middlebury.edu/index.php?action=site&site=psci0236a-f06 (August 22, 2008).

Millet, Richard. *Guardians of the Dynasty*. Maryknoll, NY: Orbis Books, 1977.

Miranda, Roger, and William Ratliff. *The Civil War in Nicaragua*. New Brunswick, NJ: Transaction Publishers, 1993.

Nolan, David. *The Ideology of the Sandinistas and the Nicaraguan Revolution*. Coral Gables, FL: Institute of Interamerican Studies, 1985.

North, Oliver. "Oliver North Quotes." *Brainyquote*. 2007. http://www.brainyquote.com/quotes/authors/o/oliver_north.html (August 22, 2008).

PBS. "Ronald Reagan's Life." *American Experience*. 1999–2000. http://www.pbs.org/wgbh/amex/reagan/timeline/index_5.html (August 22, 2008).

Pezzullo, Lawrence, and Ralph Pezzullo. *At the Fall of Somoza*. Pittsburgh: University of Pittsburgh Press, 1993.

Ponvert, Phyllis. "Nicaragua Elections, American Style." *University of Michigan*. December 2001–January 2002. http://www-personal.umich.edu/~lormand/agenda/0112/nicaragua.htm (August 22, 2008).

Randall, Margaret. *Sandino's Daughter Revisited*. New Brunswick, NJ: Rutgers University Press, 1994.

Reagan, Ronald. "Creators of the Future." *Conservative Political Action Committee*. 2006. http://www.conservative.org/pressroom/reagan/reagan1985.asp (August 22, 2008).

Rosset, Peter, and John Vandermeer, eds., *Nicaragua: Unfinished Revolution*. New York: Grove Press, 1986.

Ryan, David. *U.S.-Sandinista Diplomatic Relations*. New York: St. Martin's Press, 1995.

Sklar, Holly. *Washington's War on Nicaragua*. Boston: South End Press, 1988.

Vanden, Harry E., and Gary Prevost. *Democracy and Socialism in Sandinista Nicaragua*. Boulder, CO: Lynne Reinner Publications, 1993.

Walker, Thomas W. *Nicaragua: Living in the Shadow of the Eagle*. Boulder, CO: Westview Press, 2003.

———, ed. *Nicaragua: The First Five Years*. New York: Praeger, 1985.

———, ed. *Reagan Versus the Sandinistas*. Boulder, CO: Westview Press, 1987.

———. *Revolution & Counterrevolution in Nicaragua*. Boulder, CO: Westview Press, 1992.

Zimmerman, Matilde. *Sandinista Carlos Fonseca and the Nicaraguan Revolution*. Durham, NC: Duke University Press, 2000.

Further Reading and Websites

Books

Camardella, Michele L. *America in the 1980s.* New York: Facts on File, 2006.

Dall, Christopher. *Nicaragua in Pictures.* Minneapolis: Twenty-First Century Books, 2007.

Hines, Janet. *Inside America's CIA: The Central Intelligence Agency.* New York: Rosen, 2003.

Miller, Debra A. *Nicaragua.* San Diego: Lucent Books, 2005.

Petersen, Christine. *The Iran-Contra Scandal.* New York: Children's Press, 2004.

Schlesinger, Arthur M., Jr., ed. *The Election of 1980 and the Administration of Ronald Reagan.* Philadelphia: Mason Crest Publishers, 2003.

Videos

Connolly, Bob. *Nicaragua: No Pasaran.* DVD. Produced and directed by David Bradbury. 1984; Wilsons Creek, Australia: Frontline Films, 2003. Australian filmmaker David Bradbury spent six months in Nicaragua in the early 1980s filming the early years of the Sandinista revolutionary government as seen through the eyes of leading Sandinista Tomás Borge. Footage includes political speeches, street rallies, and other events.

Websites

Envío Digital

http://www.envio.org.ni/archivo.en

Envío is an independent pro-Sandinista magazine first published in February 1981. After the FSLN's defeat in February 1990, *Envío* began covering the rest of Central America, touching on themes such as north-south relations, neoliberalism, globalization, the women's movement, ecology, and foreign debt. In 2003 more than twenty years of editions were made available in English on the Internet. These texts are perhaps the most complete public documentation of what happened in Nicaragua in the 1980s.

Iran-Contra Affair: 20 Years On
http://www.gwu.edu/~nsarchiv/NSAEBB/NSAEBB210/index.htm
This site is run by the National Security Archive, an independent nongovernmental research institute and library located at George Washington University. It features official documents that spotlight the role of Ronald Reagan and his top aides in the Iran-Contra affair, including White House briefings, minutes of meetings, and memoranda from key players.

Nicaragua News
http://www.einnews.com/nicaragua
This website features articles, editorials, and current events of concern to Nicaraguans. Revised daily, the site provides up-to-date information about the economy, government and politics, international relations, and arts and entertainment in Nicaragua.

The Sandinista Revolution
http://www.vianica.com/go/specials/15-sandinista-revolution-in-nicaragua.html
This site provides the historical background to the Sandinista revolution, with links to present-day events in Nicaragua including headlines, nature, culture, and other information.

The Sandino Rebellion in Nicaragua, 1927–1934
http://www.sandinorebellion.com
This site is perhaps the world's largest private archive on the Sandino rebellion in Nicaragua. It features an extensive collection with thousands of documents the author has collected over a period of twenty years from archives in the United States and Nicaragua. These letters, notes, orders, diaries, prayers, lists, drafts, receipts, certificates, songs, and poems—many captured by the marines and the guardia during offensive operations—provide profound insight and put a human face on this historical event.

Index

Photo Acknowledgments

The images in this book are used with the permission of: © Bettmann/CORBIS, pp. 5, 24; © Laura Westlund/Independent Picture Service, p. 10; National Archives (NWDNS-127-EX-1-6), p. 13; Keystone/Eyedea/Everett Collection, p. 14; AP Photo, pp. 21, 26, 53, 95; © John Giannini/Sygma/CORBIS, p. 33; © AFP/Getty Images, p. 34; © Patrick Chauvel/Sygma/CORBIS, p. 37; © Alain Keler/Sygma/CORBIS, p. 44; © Jenny Matthews/Alamy, p. 46; © Cindy Karp/Time & Life Pictures/Getty Images, pp. 65, 96, 100, 107; © John Hoagland/Liaison/Getty Images, pp. 66, 73; AP Photo/Raul de Molina, p. 77; © Bill Gentile/CORBIS, pp. 83, 92; AP Photo/Scott Applewhite, p. 88; © Bill Gentile/ZUMA Press, p. 108; © Matias Recart/AFP/Getty Images, p. 114; © Lou Dematteis/The Image Works, p. 117; AP Photo/Brennan Linsley, p. 122; © Keith Dannemiller/ZUMA Press, p. 126; AP Photo/Esteban Felix, p. 130.

Front Cover: © Matthew Naythons/Getty Images.

About the Author

Stuart A. Kallen has written more than 250 nonfiction books for children and young adults over the past twenty years. His books have covered countless aspects of human history, culture, and science from the building of the pyramids to the music of the twenty-first century. Kallen is also an accomplished singer-songwriter and guitarist in San Diego, California.